PRAISE FOR
THE LONELY CHILD

"A splendid book, reflecting the author's determination to learn about her missing family. It is an endearing story told with a crisp writing style that will hold the reader's attention to the very end."

> -Bernard F. Conners, British American Publishing,
> and Former Publisher of *The Paris Review*

"Heartache and disappointment are well-balanced with humor and joy in this riveting, always truthful story. Moyer's refreshing voice identifies the needs and rights of all those who share this journey: one we don't often hear, but need to."

> -Elizabeth Osta, author of *Jeremiah's Hunger* and
> *Saving Faith: A Memoir of Courage,*
> *Conviction, and a Calling*

THE

LONELY

CHILD

THE

LONELY

CHILD

*THE JOURNEY OF SEARCH
TO FIND MY BIOLOGICAL FAMILY*

SUSAN MOYER

Tranquil Waters Books

ROCHESTER, NY

Cover design by Rachael Gootnick
Layout by Nina Alvarez

For permission to reprint portions of this book,
or to order a review copy, contact:
susanmoyerauthor@gmail.com

ISBN-13: 978-0-692-12507-6

Dedicated in loving memory

of

Bryce James Moyer

and

Ava Priscilla Moyer

And in dedication to my family and friends,
who have been by my side throughout this long
journey, and to all those who are still searching.

CONTENTS

"In all of us there is a hunger marrow-deep, to know our heritage—
to know who we are and where we have come from.
Without this enriching knowledge, there is a hollow yearning.
No matter what our attainments in life, there is still a vacuum,
emptiness, and the most disquieting loneliness."

–Alex Haley, *Roots*

"The final mystery is oneself."

–Oscar Wilde, *De Profundis*

PROLOGUE

There is an old expression that goes something like: "If you don't know where you came from, then you don't know where you're going."

Hundreds of thousands of adoptees have no idea where they came from—how they came to be or who was involved. I was one of them. I wanted—needed—to find the answers to all my unanswered questions: Who were my biological parents? Why did they give me up for adoption? Who did I look like? Did I have siblings? Throughout my life, I had this overpowering feeling that something was amiss. There was a void in my life, and I was compelled to discover what it was, what caused it, and how to fill it.

I had no idea how my story would unfold or where it would lead me. My search for answers took me back to

Albany, the place of my birth, to walking the streets of Brooklyn, to the bowels of Manhattan, to Toronto and even Ireland. I felt that anything I discovered along the way would add to the missing pieces of my own personal puzzle.

Searching for one's biological family can be a long and lonely journey. Even with the support of family and friends, what you are searching for is very personal and most meaningful to you and you alone.

Regardless of what lay ahead as I ventured into the unknown, I knew that I needed to go back to the beginning—my beginning—in hopes of discovering who I was and why.

Everyone has a story; this just happens to be mine.

THE GIRL AT THE WINDOW

She is there again, as on many Sunday afternoons. The young girl stands vigilant and in total solitude by the window. Her back is to me. It appears that she is straining to see through the sheer, cream-colored curtain. I stare at her long, light hair gently hanging down over her shoulders. Not a muscle is moving, so focused is she on whatever is outside the window.

I stand behind and watch as her slender hand gracefully reaches up and touches the stiff, faded fabric. She pulls it aside ever so gently . . . then, without warning, her fingers let the material fall back into place as though her presence could be detected with any movement at all. This is her vantage point where she can observe and not be seen. This is her window into a world she longs to be a part of, but isn't.

Suddenly her body stiffens. She seems to sense she is not alone. Slowly and deliberately she turns her head and looks directly at me. I freeze. My heart skips a beat.

Oh God, I know this young girl. Those sad and lonely eyes . . . the tears—oh, how I know those tears.

THE BEGINNING OF THE END

It is Sunday, October 26, 2008, a beautiful crystal-clear fall day in New York City. There have been many days similar to this before, but yet none quite like today. The sky is a brilliant cerulean blue, the temperature is warm—seventy degrees—and the sun is peering down between the giant concrete and glass buildings that make up the skyline of Manhattan. I rush around our apartment trying to prepare myself for an afternoon dinner at my favorite restaurant, Scalinatella. Before heading out for the four-block walk up Third Avenue, I take one last glance in the mirror. Staring at my reflection, I am feeling anything but confident in what I see. But after three wardrobe changes, time has run out. I really need to get going.

My final selection will just have to do: black slacks, a black turtleneck—a standard in my wardrobe—and a tur-

quoise jacket with matching jewelry. My hands are trembling so much I'm having a terrible time just trying to put
my earrings on. Oh God, I think, I just want everything
to be perfect.

I pause to take a deep breath. Trying to control my
nerves is futile, but I say to myself that this is it: time to
head out the door for one of the most important days of
my life.

Scalinatella is located below the cacophony of the
streets of Manhattan. As you walk down the staircase
that leads into the restaurant, the first thing you notice
are wonderful aromas of garlic and fresh herbs. They per-
meate the air. The place has a warm, intimate, inviting
atmosphere. Dim recessed lighting and gray stone- walls
give you the feeling that you have just entered a Tuscan
grotto.

Arriving at the restaurant, I am affectionately greeted by our host, Johnny, who I have known for years. His

wonderful smile and friendly demeanor help to calm my jitters. Johnny has come in early to oversee the dinner and to make sure everything will go as planned. I notice the bartender is already waiting to serve the first of the many cocktails that will be needed to get through this day. A little liquid courage certainly wouldn't hurt right now.

My wonderful husband, Paul, has made all the arrangements. He is here with me along with my sons, Jeffrey and Jason. Someone else who has become an important part of my life over the past three years is also with me today.

I look around the room. Along one of the stone-walls, a long table is set with a white tablecloth and adorned with small vases of pale-colored flowers. The table is set for thirteen; thirteen members of my family are coming together. Who would have thought? I am in awe. I will finally be having the large family dinner I always dreamt of but never imagined would become a reality. As I glance around the room at the people here with me, I smile. An indescribable warmth floods my heart. I am, surrounded by family. Sometimes people take family for granted, but I never do.

We are all standing around anxiously awaiting the arrival of our other guests: people I have never seen or spoken to before. These are complete strangers with whom I have a special bond. These individuals did not even know of my existence four short weeks ago. They will be arriving any minute, and when they do, it will be time to celebrate. Who would have thought that after twenty-plus years of searching this day would come? Where do we go from here? How will this all turn out? What happens next?

Today I do not have the answers and that is okay, because I feel such gratitude and jubilation. Somehow I have accomplished—seemingly—the impossible.

WHERE IT BEGAN

Her life began on the evening on October 12, 1953, at Brady Maternity Hospital, Albany, New York. A woman gave birth to a little girl and named her Susan Ann. No last name was given, for shortly after giving birth, the birth mother requested then signed adoption papers relinquishing all rights to the child.

Five days later, Susan Ann was moved to an adjacent building, an orphanage called St. Catherine's Infant Home, which was run by Roman Catholic nuns, The Daughters of Charity. This was now her home, along with many other children waiting to be adopted. Susan was officially an orphan.

She would retain no memories of her time at St. Catherine's, but this was the place where she slept, where someone fed her and changed her diapers, and where someone possibly held and soothed her when she cried.

In April of the following year, a couple came to St. Catherine's. They were seven years into marriage and still childless. All the necessary paperwork and background checks were completed, and although a son is what they wanted, Susan was the one they chose.

They endured months of weekly nerve-racking visits from social workers checking in to see how the prospective parents were coping and how Baby Susan was adjusting. On May 27, 1955, at nineteen months old, the adoption was finalized through Catholic Charities, and Susan legally became their daughter. She knew nothing of her adoption. It remained a secret for sixteen years. But as with most things, the truth eventually comes out.

Susan learning that she was adopted was just the beginning of what would become a lifelong journey. She had no idea what lay ahead in discovering the story behind her adoption. She knew nothing of all the events, the people she would encounter, or the stories and the lives that she would be touched by throughout the process.

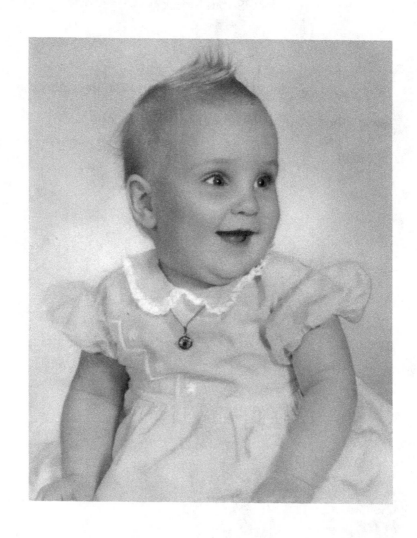

THE LONELY CHILD

My adoptive parents were both born and raised in Boston, Massachusetts. Both were educated, from large families, and survivors of the Great Depression. Shortly after the start of World War II, both of them enlisted in the service: my father in the Army, and my mother in the Marines. Needless to say, I grew up in a very disciplined household.

Within a year of my adoption being finalized, my parents packed up everything they owned and moved out of the Albany area to Syracuse, New York. I had a pretty typical middle-class childhood. I was raised Catholic and attended a parochial elementary school. Each morning during my six years at St. Rose of Lima, I would head out the door in my ugly school uniform: a maroon jumper with a white Peter Pan–collared shirt. The school was run by an order of Franciscan nuns. At the time, the nuns wore black and white habits with only their hands and faces visible. Everything else from head to toe was covered. I noticed that sometimes little wisps of hair would peek out around their faces. I was fascinated that they actually had hair; I had thought nuns had to shave their heads. To complete their ensemble was a white cowl or what I thought of as a very large bib, and when they moved a certain way, a white T-shirt was exposed, just like the kind my father wore. Around their waists, each wore a white rope with three knots and the largest rosary beads I had ever seen.

The majority of the nuns did not radiate warmth; their motto was to instill "the fear of God" into each and every one of us. I was terrified of them. Back then it was perfectly normal for a nun to actually strike a child when misbehaving. They would either use a yardstick, a ruler, or the infamous pointer that always sat on the ledge of the large, green dusty chalkboard. The ruler seemed to be their weapon of choice, used to smack a child's knuckles—and let me tell you, it hurt like hell. I remember getting smacked when I had folded my hands in prayer incorrectly. My little fingers were supposed to be pressed tightly together and pointed up to the heavens, but I had left spaces between my fingers "allowing the devil to get in."

My original perception of nuns was that they were not human. I am not sure what I thought they were. It wasn't until one day when I was in the fifth grade and one of the nuns, Sister John Francis, asked me to wait outside the adult restroom. While I stood out in the hallway contemplating what she was doing, I suddenly figured out that she must be human if she went to the bathroom. A true revelation!

A part of my Catholic upbringing was to make my First Holy Communion. Before you were allowed to do that, you had to make your First Penance, where you go to confession and tell a priest your sins. As a young child, this is daunting. You enter a confessional—basically a closet in the back of the church—where you kneel down and wait for the priest to slide open a screen that separates you and then he asks you to tell your sins. After reciting the opening line of "Bless me, Father, for I have sinned," you proceed to confess your sins—for example, "I disobeyed my mother three times." The priest would then give you penance for your sins: "Say three Acts of Contrition, four Our Fathers, and three Hail Marys. After doing so, you are absolved from your sins and able to accept Holy Communion."

My mother once shared a story with me about an evening when she went to my first grade parents' night. On entering the classroom, the nuns warmly greeted her and instantly congratulated her for just having a baby. I cannot imagine the shock and the look of horror on my mother's face and the explanation that must have followed, for of course she did not just have a baby. I had gone to school and made up the story, for I so desperately wanted a brother or sister. I am not sure, considering my age at the time and the severity of the lie I told, if it was a mortal or venial sin? You may have to be Catholic to understand the specific levels of sin that we were taught, one being far worse than the other. But I do believe that due to my age, I will not be sent directly to Hell for that particular tale.

I was simply envious that all of my friends had brothers and sisters. I was the "lonely child," for that is how I referred to myself when asked if I had any brothers or sisters. Of course I should have said "only child," but "lonely" was the word I always used. My house seemed like the quietest, most boring house in the neighborhood. There was just me, my parents, and whatever pet we had at the time.

What I did have waiting for me at home were my dolls. I loved my dolls; they were my surrogate siblings. I had baby dolls, Ginny dolls, Madame Alexander dolls, and Barbie dolls, all with names I had specifically chosen. I would sit in my bedroom and spend hours dressing and undressing them with the utmost care. I would have fabulous conversations with each. I spoke to them and it seemed to me that they spoke back. My mother said that she would stand outside my room listening to my conversations. If she hadn't known better, she would have thought I had a room full of friends, and for me I did.

Do I believe that I mistakenly always used the word "lonely" instead of "only child" when referring to myself? I do not believe so. For lonely child was certainly how I felt about myself. When I became a young adolescent, I remember asking my mother: Why she never had any other children. What had happened to her maternity clothes? What was it like to have a baby? Not untypical questions coming from an inquisitive young girl. To this day, I remember feeling quite unsatisfied with the vague answers my mother would give.

Although, at this point in my life I had not been told that I was adopted, I remember having classmates in school who were adopted and it wasn't anything to be ashamed of. One friend in particular was adopted and her parents adopted several children. It was something that was celebrated—apparently just not when it came to me.

The older I got, the taller I grew. "You're growing like a weed," people would say to me. I hated it. I did not look at all like my parents, or like anyone for that matter. My parents were short with dark hair and here I was, tall with green eyes and medium-blond hair. My friends looked like members of their families, so why didn't I?

I remember crying and telling my mother many times that I wanted to have surgery to make me shorter. When I think of that, it speaks volumes to how out of place and different I felt about myself. My mother's response was always the same: practical, but ignoring the point, skirting the much deeper issue.

I wanted to be five-foot-two with eyes of blue like other girls. I will never understand, knowing how miserable I was, why my mother still would not tell me the truth: that I was adopted. I know that it would have made such a difference in how I felt about myself. I suffered with such low self-esteem, being so tall and thin, unlike anyone around me. To make matters worse, starting in the second grade I had to wear glasses; without them I could not see a foot in front of me. Back then the term "four-eyes" was used by children to mock anyone who wore spectacles— and there I was with my horned-rimmed glasses.

The question of why was I so different was something I constantly asked myself. I would slouch when standing in the church pew next to my parents in the pew so that I would not tower above them, something that has affected my posture to this day. At one point, my mother had me wear a back brace to hold my shoulders back to try to correct my posture. Every day I would be told to stand up straight, and every day I would try to make myself look shorter. And when it came to family photos, forget it. Being forced to stand next to my parents and smile was pure torture.

I absolutely hated being that "lonely child." To fill the void in my life I even created imaginary people. A therapist would have had a field day with that. When my mother and I would drive into the city from the suburbs for a day of shopping, I would have her pretend to pull over and pick up a couple of friends to join us. I had even created an imaginary family. There were parents, an older brother and a younger one, and a younger sister. Each had a name, but most importantly, all were tall and looked like me. I even designed the house we lived in, right down to the color of the walls. Each night in bed, while I was trying to fall asleep, I would escape to my imaginary world and the family I had created. I had a wonderful feeling of peace and belonging there. I was no longer the misfit.

I was often told I had a vivid imagination, but no one knew just how vivid.

I desperately needed to identify with someone on a physical and emotional level. But who would understand? *I* didn't even understand. What was this feeling of emptiness, of loneliness, that seemed to consume me? All I wanted was to have a family exactly like the one living next door. On Sunday afternoons, the grandparents, aunts and uncles, parents and children would all gather together for dinner. I know this because I was the girl—the one standing alone like a sentinel by the window—peering through the sheer, cream-colored curtain, wishing I could be one of them.

KINDERGARTEN

THE BIG SECRET EXPOSED

When I entered the tumultuous teenage years, everything seemed to be changing and I really began to question who I was and where I came from. I had a wonderful relationship with my cousins in Boston and would spend time with them each summer without my parents. Pat and Bob lived right on the water and I loved the smell of the salt air and going out on their boat exploring Boston Harbor. I had a great sense of freedom being there. When I was around fifteen years old, I began to verbalize and share my deep-rooted feelings with my cousins. I confided that I believed that I was adopted; in fact, I was positive of it.

The summer before my sixteenth birthday, my cousin Pat finally had heard enough and decided it was time to call my mother. She told my mother that I was quite sure I was adopted, and it was time she told me the truth.

It was not Pat's place to tell me, it needed to come from my parents.

The day of reckoning finally happened in the fall right before my sixteenth birthday. I am convinced the only reason my parents were going to expose the BIG SECRET at that point was because of the call from Pat, and because I was hounding my parents about getting my driving permit, for which I needed a birth certificate.

My mother told me that she and my father wanted to sit down together and have a talk with me. I was racking my brain trying to figure out why I was in trouble. What on earth had I done wrong to have to be summoned to a meeting with both of my parents? I remember thinking that this couldn't be good.

So it was on a Saturday morning when my parents called me into the living room and told me to sit down, they had something they needed to tell me. My father was sitting in his chair by the window where he always sat. My mother was perched on the end of the brown floral couch, and I took my place at the opposite end of the couch nearest the door, just in case I needed to make a quick exit. The muted morning sunlight was peeking through the gold drapes that hung over the large picture window.

The room was filled with a sort of eerie yellowish hue, looking almost like a sepia photograph. I remember the conversation starting with my mother telling me that both she and my father loved me. That is the only time I was ever told that.

My mother then proceeded. They had found out after seven years of marriage that they could not have children and so they decided to adopt. I was the child they adopted.

There it was. They finally said it to me after sixteen years: "You are adopted."

Because I had already known in my heart that I was adopted, it did not come as any great shock. But I will admit that I felt vindicated and said to myself, "I knew it!" This explanation finally made clear to me why I looked different, but did it explain the void I felt?

My mother went on to say how special I was because I was chosen. Funny, I did not feel special.

This is the motto that adoptive parents seem to have been told by adoption agencies to tell an adoptive child. Although true—I was indeed chosen—the phrase did not mean anything to me. Back then and to this day still doesn't. I am not sure why, other than the fact that for sixteen years I wasn't told the truth. Could it be that if they had been honest from the beginning—had made me feel that it was something wonderful instead of something to be ashamed of—I would feel differently about myself?

My father sat there, barely uttering a word. My mother went on to say that when we moved to central New York from Albany, they decided not to tell anyone, including me, that I was adopted. It was for my "own protection." She said, "People can be cruel and we didn't want you to feel different."

I guess they hadn't been listening every time I told them how different I felt. So different, in fact, that I would come to them in tears asking to have surgery to make me shorter so that I would fit in.

They should have told me from the beginning. I should have grown up with the knowledge that I was adopted. Who were they trying to protect? Themselves?

I will always disagree with their decision. I feel strongly about that for any adoptee. Everyone has a right to know where they came from.

"Do you have any questions?" my mother asked.

What? Of course I had questions.

"Who were my parents? Did I have brothers or sisters?"

She said they didn't have any information other than that my birth mother was Irish and had decided that she could not keep me and that putting me up for adoption would be best. My mother did add that she had been told that my birth mother had hesitated and almost didn't sign the adoption papers. I was told that I was born in Brady Maternity Hospital in Albany and then put in St. Catherine's Infant Home where my parents found me. My mother said that I was a healthy, happy baby. The only thing I would do at night laying in my crib was rock so hard in fact, that I would move my crib across the hardwood floor. I now know that was a way to self-soothe, a way to comfort myself, and something that I would continue to do into adulthood when trying to fall asleep. Is it because there was no one in the orphanage to rock me? Was no one there to hold me? I was, after all, only one child in an institution filled with many others.

My mother then said that it was up to me if I wanted to tell anyone that I was adopted. I am sure they were praying that I would continue to keep their BIG SE-

CRET. Of course it would be a scary thought for them if I told anyone and it got back to their friends—then they'd really have a lot of explaining to do.

The tension in the room was palpable. The three of us just sat there motionless, waiting for one another to speak. My father nervously lit his third cigarette and my mother looked like she was going to be ill. My recollection is that only an hour had passed since the conversation started, although it was beginning to feel like an eternity. Though this conversation was long overdue, or perhaps because it was, I was anxious to get out of that room, that house. I couldn't get away from my parents fast enough.

I asked if I could be excused and go next door to my best friend Kathy's house. My mother gave her permission. Before leaving I asked if getting my birth certificate meant that I could get my driving permit, and that too was a "yes." I was now a full-fledged teenager who would be able to get behind the wheel of a car. I thought that was pretty awesome.

In addition to being able to drive, I had recently purchased my first pair of contact lenses. No more "four eyes" for me. Also, my mother allowed a friend to pierce my ears. It was done the old-fashioned way: with ice cubes to numb my earlobes followed by a giant sewing needle inserted through my earlobe. That hurt! But for me it was well worth it. I'd do anything to feel better about myself.

The most important thing that ever happened to me was being told I was adopted. I was now going to see my birth certificate for the first time. I soon discovered, however, that it was not my original birth certificate. It is called an amended birth certificate, which is what adoptive parents receive at the time they adopt a child. This birth certificate has their names on it, not the birth parents' names. The original is kept on file with the State. At this point it would take An Act of God to ever get hold of. My birth records for now will remain, permanently sealed.

I am certain that my parents were terrified that I would expose their secret. I also think they must have thought to themselves that I took the news pretty well. Again, what they shared with me was not surprising. It was an affirmation of what I already believed to be true. I do not know how they felt after. I am sure they were scared, maybe a little relieved.

After being excused, I ran next door as fast as I could and found Kathy sitting alone in her musty basement. She looked up at me as I came down the stairs, and within the first five minutes of my arrival, I blurted out what I had just learned: "I'm adopted."

Well, that certainly didn't take me long. For all the years my parents had been keeping their BIG SECRET, I had exposed it in fewer than five minutes. I just didn't understand why it was a secret in the first place.

Kathy's reaction: "Oh, I knew it! My mother told me

that she thought you might be adopted."

Kathy somehow just always knew everything. She was wiser than the rest of us. While the two of us just sat there, staring at each other contemplating what this revelation meant, her transistor radio was playing "Yesterday" by the Beatles.

To this day, whenever I hear that song, that exact moment in time is clearly etched in my memory.

IDENTIFYING OR NON-IDENTIFYING

My life did not change in any earth-shattering way. Nor was I immediately traumatized by my parents' revelation regarding my adoption. Although, throughout my life, there have been residual effects. The topic continued to be a subject never to be discussed, at least with my parents. They never mentioned it. Of course I did not keep their secret. I didn't have a problem telling people that I was adopted. To my knowledge none of my parents' friends ever found out, and if they did, they kept it to themselves.

When I was eighteen, I drove to Albany to visit a favorite aunt of mine, my mother's sister, who was dying of cancer. I remember realizing at the time that I was driving to the city where I was born. I arrived at the hospital and entered my aunt's room. It was sad to see how frail she was. I took the seat next to her bed and we made small talk. After about a half hour, I told her that I had been told the truth and now knew that I was adopted. She said that she was glad my parents had finally told me. She said that my mother's greatest fear was that after finding out I was adopted, I would feel that she wasn't my real mother and that I wouldn't have to obey or listen to her.

Even as a rebellious teenager, that never crossed my mind. She was, and is to this day, the only mother I have ever known. Giving birth to a child does not define what a mother is. It is the lifetime of commitment, caring, support, and unconditional love that makes someone a mother.

Years later, at my father's funeral in Boston, I was speaking with my father's brother and told him that I knew that I was adopted. He too was happy that my parents had told me the truth, and he thought it was wrong of them not to tell me from the beginning.

Throughout my twenties I would continue to ponder where I came from, always wondering, *Who are my birth parents? Do I have siblings? Who do I look like?* These are all normal thoughts anyone would have if they didn't have the answers.

Each year on my birthday, I would especially wonder if my birth mother ever thought of me. There have been several times in my life when someone would say to me that I looked like someone they knew. When in public, I would always scan the faces in a crowd, seeking some similarity and wondering if any were possibly related.

I went to school, worked hard, and built a career in advertising and radio. My life was moving right along.

In 1978, I met my future husband, Paul. We were married in March of 1980 and moved to Rochester, New York: Paul's hometown and the location of his business. Paul had been married before, divorced for quite a few years, and had two children. So along with adjusting to married life and a new city, I became a stepmother to a nine-year-old and a thirteen-year-old. I knew absolutely nothing about raising children. How could I? I was twenty-eight and went from single to married with children in one fell swoop.

I think back to that period in my life now and have no idea how I did it. Luckily, my stepchildren were great and I am happy to say that thirty-eight years later, I still have a wonderful relationship with them.

In March of 1981 I discovered that we were expecting our first child. I called my parents to give them the joyful news. They seemed to be thrilled, but I felt sad for them. My mother never experienced what I was experiencing: she'd never given birth.

My first son, Jeffrey Paul, arrived on December 5, which just happened to be Paul's birthday—quite the gift. And for me, for the first time in my life, I was looking at my own flesh and blood.

I remember so clearly holding my beautiful newborn son, checking him over from head to toe, making sure he had everything he was suppose to have. Paul and I stared at his little scrunched-up face trying to determine whom he looked like. I was so hoping that there would be some resemblance to me.

Jeffrey had dark hair that stood out all over his head. I looked up at Paul and said, "Really, he *is* yours!" Everyone in Paul's family have blond hair and blue eyes. I proudly realized that someone in *my* family must have dark hair!

When you are not adopted, you would not think of something like that, but this moment was incredible for me on so many levels. I was lying on the delivery table, holding my precious son as Paul stood by me, grinning from ear to ear. He said, "This is the best birthday present ever."

Suddenly the doctor and nurses erupted into song, singing "Happy Birthday" to Paul—and I guess to Jeffrey

Paul too.

And it truly was a happy birthday.

On September 27, 1984, I gave birth to our second son, Jason. Once again, as I did with Jeffrey, I held Jason and looked at him in wonder. Another human being to whom I was blood related. I now had two children and they were the only people on Earth that I knew were my flesh and blood. Jason was beautiful, almost nine pounds, with light blond hair. This time Paul did not question his parentage.

After Jason's birth, I once again started wondering where I came from and what I was passing on to my children. I now had two special reasons why I should try to find out who I came from. Back then, few people had personal computers and there was no such thing as the internet. The only way to communicate or do any form of research was by telephone and mail. Somehow I discovered that New York State had recently created a couple of

new programs called Identifying and Non-Identifying information. These programs were made available for adoptees to obtain information regarding their adoptions. I
decided that this was where I would begin the search for
my biological family.

I called the New York Vital Statistics Bureau to request the forms I needed. Within a week I received a
letter and the forms. Of course I wanted Identifying information, but in order to receive it, one needed the permission of all parties involved. That included the birth
parents, the adoptive parents, and the birth child. Well,
that seemed ridiculous. If I had all that information, why
would I need the State of New York's help? I certainly
was not about to approach my adoptive parents to get
their permission. I was doing this on my own. This was
my BIG SECRET from them, and just one of many to
come regarding my adoption.

Having to settle for the Non-Identifying information,

which did not require anyone's permission, I carefully answered the list of questions with what little information I had about myself and mailed it back to the State. Now all I could do was wait and see. Within a couple of weeks, I received a letter informing me that the State had received my paperwork and working on my case.

Well, at least I now had a case.

A month later, an official-looking envelope arrived in the mail from the New York State Adoption Registry. This was it. This is what I had been waiting for.

With much anticipation, I tore open the envelope and started to read. It was in column form. On the left side was the information for the birth mother and on the right information regarding the birth father. There were an awful lot of empty spaces, meaning that the State was sharing very little.

It stated that my mother was a divorcée and felt that it was best for her child to be placed for adoption.

It stated that she was twenty-nine years old at the time of my birth, Irish and Canadian, Roman Catholic, an office worker. A little further down it stated that she was extremely pretty, very friendly, and a well set-up person.

What the hell did that mean? A well set-up person? I had no idea. But I kept going back to the part that said she was pretty. I never felt pretty or even attractive, so to read that my birth mother was pretty for some reason made me happy. Wet salty spots appeared on the paper I held as tears ran down my face. I quickly dabbed my eyes with my sleeve for fear of smearing the ink on the valuable document. My eyes glanced over to the right side of the paper under birth father. There was even less information there. It stated that he was between the ages of twenty-four and twenty-seven, Irish, a high school graduate, and a truck driver.

Paul was out of town in Vermont on business that day, but I really wanted to speak with him. This was before the age of cell phones, so I called the emergency number Paul had left. Okay, so it wasn't exactly an emergency, but I didn't care. I dialed the number and listened impatiently while I heard the rotary phone slowly dialing each number. Clickkkkaa, clickkkaa. It seemed to go on forever.

When it stopped and actually started to ring, I heard a man finally answer and say, "Hello?"

Trying to control the excitement in my voice, I said, "Hi, my name is Susan Moyer, Paul's wife. Is it possible to speak with Paul? It's not an emergency but it is very important."

He told me to hold on while he went and got Paul.

"Hi, what's wrong?" Paul asked as soon as he got on the phone.

I told him everyone was fine, and then I proceeded in one long breath to tell him the reason for my call. "I just received the information from the State." I shared with him what was on the form, and when it came to the part that said my mother was "pretty," I really choked up.

I was now holding in my hands the first information that I ever received about my biological parents. I was hoping it would tell me that my mother was tall or provide a more descriptive detail of her physically. And surely the State would have told me if I had siblings . . . right? After all, that wasn't Identifying information. I was sure that if I had siblings they would have said. Did this mean that I did not have any brothers or sisters?

Now what? Where would I go from here? Was this all that I would ever learn about my birth parents? Was this the end of my journey?

CUMMING TOWER   THE GOVERNOR NELSON A. ROCKEFELLER EMPIRE STATE PLAZA   ALBANY, N.Y 12237

DAVID AXELROD, M.D.
Commissioner

LINDA A. RANDOLPH, M.D., M.P.H.
Director

WILLIAM F. LEAVY
Executive Deputy Director

CONFIDENTIAL   November 14, 1986

Ms. Susan F. Moyer

Registry #_____

Dear Ms. Moyer:

We are continuing to process your application for non-identifying information.

Currently, we are waiting for information from the Adoption Agency which handled your adoption. In accordance with the current law, the Adoption Agency may charge a fee up to $50.00 to cover the cost of searching their records. Please contact the Agency at the address listed below regarding their billing procedures. We will notify you as soon as we receive the information from the agency.

If you requested identifying information, it may be released only if the Registry receives the registration and consent of all three parties to your adoption. If your adoptive parent(s) are deceased a certified copy of the death certificate(s) must be filed with the Registry. If you have not already done so, please send the certified copies of the death certificate(s) immediately.

If I can be of further assistance, please do not hesitate to contact me.

Sincerely,

Stephen M. Sherokey
Public Health Representative
NYS Adoption Information Registry

```
Adoption Agency
Community Maternity Services
27 North Main Avenue
Albany, New York    12203
Ms. Mary Creighton
```

PROCESSING – APPLICATION

COMMUNITY MATERNITY SERVICES

February 20, 1987

Mrs. Susan Moyer

Dear Susan,

We have received your Registration Form requesting non-identifying information which we are enclosing herewith. We are required to send a copy of the Registration to New York State Adoption Information Registry along with the non-identifying information. That agency may have additional data for you and you should hear from them in the next few weeks.

For the sake of clarification, Susan, you were born at Brady Maternity Hospital in Albany (now closed) and you were placed at St. Catherine Infant Home on October 17, 1953. On April 23, 1954 Catholic Charities placed you for adoption in the home of   and   . All matters pertaining to adoption are now handled by Community Maternity Services.

You were baptized at the Infant Home Chapel (St. Catherine) on October 23, 1953. Should you ever need a record of your baptism, you would write to the Chancery Office, 465 State Street, Albany, N.Y. 12203.

We hope the enclosed information will be helpful to you. Please feel free to be in touch if we can be of further assistance.

Sincerely, yours,

Helen T. Dunigan, C.S.W.
Adoption Archivist

___ ADMINISTRATION
27 North Main Avenue
Albany, New York 12203
(518) 482-8836

___ MATERNITY CENTER
29 North Main Avenue
Albany, New York 12203
(518) 482-6836

___ BRANSON FAMILY DEVELOPM.
CENTER
31 North Main Avenue
Albany, New York 12203
(518) 482-8836

___ ADOPTION AND FOSTER CARE
27 North Main Avenue
Albany, New York 12203
(518) 482-8836

___ FAMILY LIFE EDUCATION
27 North Main Avenue
Albany, New York 12203
(518) 482-8836

___ SCHOHARIE COUNTY
41 West Main Street
Cobleskill, New York 12043
(518) 234-2841

___ OTSEGO COUNTY
39 Walnut Street
Oneonta, New York 12820
(607) 432-9930

___ INFANT HEALTH ASSESSMENT
PROGRAM
41 West Main Street
Cobleskill, New York 12043
(518) 234-2841

___ HERKIMER COUNTY
216 Henry Street
Herkimer, New York 13350
(315) 866-6171

___ WARREN COUNTY
Lower Amherst Street
Lake George, New York 12845
(518) 695-3167

___ WASHINGTON COUNTY
79 Bulkley Avenue
Granville, New York 12832
(518) 642-1471

___ FULTON COUNTY
206 West State Street
Johnstown, New York 12095
(518) 762-6513

___ MONTGOMERY COUNTY
1 Kimball Street
Amsterdam, New York 12010
(518) 842-4202

___ RENSSELAER COUNTY
240 Second Street
Troy, New York 12180
(518) 274-9245

BAPTISM INFORMATION

STATE OF NEW YORK
DEPARTMENT OF HEALTH OFFICE OF PUBLIC HEALTH

CORNING TOWER · THE GOVERNOR NELSON A. ROCKEFELLER EMPIRE STATE PLAZA · ALBANY, N.Y. 12237

DAVID AXELROD, M.D.
Commissioner

LINDA A. RANDOLPH M.D., M.P.H.
Director

WILLIAM F. LEAVY
Executive Deputy Director

CONFIDENTIAL   March 13, 1987

Susan F. Moyer

Registry #

Dear Ms. Moyer:

Enclosed is the available non-identifying information about your biological parents and your adoption.

The Adoption Information Registry obtained this information from your original birth certificate, the records of the court, and the agency (if any) that handled your adoption.

In some cases, the available non-identifying information is rather limited. There are many situations where the biological mother declined to identify the biological father. Therefore, the records will have little or no information.

I hope that you find the information that we were able to obtain for you to be helpful. Our records indicate that non-identifying information is all that you requested. Therefore, your case is now closed. Should you at anytime wish to be registered for identifying information also, please contact us. Upon reception of your request for a status change to identifying information, we will notify you of the necessary procedures to be taken.

Thank you for participating in the New York State Adoption Information Registry.

Sincerely,

Stephen M. Sherokey
Public Health Representative
NYS Adoption Information Registry

NON-IDENTIFYING INFORMATION LETTER

Registrant's °   Susan   Moyer   *Date of Adoption:*May 27, 1955

NON-IDENTIFYING INFORMATION:
        Concerning the biological parents at the time of birth of said child.

ITEM	MOTHER	FATHER
Age	29	Not reported
Heritage:		
Nationality	Canadian born	" "
Ethnic Background	Irish	Irish-German
Race	Caucasian	Not reported
Physical Appearance:		
Height	Not reported	Not reported
Weight	" "	" "
Hair Color	" "	" "
Eye Color	" "	" "
Skin Color	" "	" "
Other Characteristics	Though not specifically recorded,	" "
	she is described as an extremely	" "
Religion	Roman Catholic [pretty woman.	" "
Education	Not reported	" "
	" "	
Occupation	Office worker	Truck driver

Interests, talents, and hobbies of biological mother The biological mother is described as a
very well set up, nice, warm and friendly person.

Interests, talents, and hobbies of biological father No interests, talents, or hobbies
reported for the biological father.

Health history of biological mother The mother has no specific recorded history, except
that there is no known history of any communicable diseases. You were treated for eczema as
an infant.

Health history of biological father No health history recorded for the biological father.

Facts and circumstances relating to the nature and cause of adoption Catholic Charities
was requested by Albany County Children's Services to place you in an adoption home.
The record simply states that the birth mother, a divorcee, was unable to keep the child.
She requested placement by an authorized agency because she felt it best for her child.
Regarding the birth, this 40 week baby was born weighing 8 pounds, 6 ounces.

NON-IDENTIFYING INFORMATION 1

Ethnic Background	Irish	Irish-German
Race	Caucasian	
Education (indicate number of school years completed)		
Physical Appearance Height	Though not specifically	Not recorded
Weight	recorded, she is des-	
Hair Color	cribed as an extremely	
Eye Color	pretty woman.	
Skin Color		
Other characteristics		
Religion	Roman Catholic	Not recorded
Occupation	Office worker	truck driver

Talents, hobbies and interests of biological mother ___ Is described as a very well set up person—a nice, warm and friendly person. Well regarded by her employer.

Talents, hobbies and interests of biological father _____ Not recorded

5. Health history of biological mother. None recorded except no known history of any communi-cable diseases. As an infant Susan was treated for eczema.

6. Health history of biological father. Non recorded.

7. Facts and circumstances relating to the nature and cause of the adoption. Catholic Charities was requested by Albany County Children's Services to place Susan in an adoption home. The record simply states the birth mother, a divorcee, was unable to keep her and she requested placement by an authorized adoption agency because she felt it best for her child.

This report was completed by:	Helen T. Dunigan, CSW	Adoption Archivist
Helen T. Dunigan		2/20/87
Name	Title	Date

NOTE: Attach additional sheets as necessary for any item(s) listed above. Please indicate the item number on the sheet(s).

NON-IDENTIFYING INFORMATION 2

NOT ALONE

My life got very busy and the next few years flew by. Between working as an advertising copywriter and radio commercial producer, and raising my sons (which is a full-time job), I did not have time to pursue my adoption search. But my interest in where I came from was never far from my mind. Every time I would see a reunion story on television where long-lost family members were reunited or meeting for the first time, I would feel envious and think, *Why couldn't that be me?*

Each year we would go to Boston to visit my family. As we were zipping down the New York State Thruway through Albany, I would always think about it being the place where my life began, and each time I would wonder if my birth mother still lived in the area.

Gradually something new had come into our lives:

the age of personal computers. What an amazing invention, especially for someone like myself who was interested in doing research. Of course, in the beginning I had no idea how to do much of anything on a computer. In fact, computers terrified me, but I made it my goal to learn to use them. The first computer that we purchased was a Tandy from Radio Shack.

In the spring of 1998, I decided the time had come once again to get back into my search for my biological family. In May, Paul was scheduled to drive to Connecticut but was stopping first in Albany for a scheduled meeting. He asked if I wanted to join him on his road trip. I decided to go, but I needed to find something to do with myself while Paul was tied up in his meeting for two hours.

Now what would I do in Albany while I waited for Paul, I wondered. Then suddenly it came to me. But did I have the courage to do it? Did I have the mettle to go through with it?

Before heading to Albany I gathered what little information I had from the State regarding my adoption. I looked up the address of what had been St. Catherine's orphanage in 1953 and headed off into the unknown. I was going to the place where it all began for me, the place of my birth.

I dropped Paul off at his meeting on Friday morning. Then, with a quick check of the map I had open on the passenger seat (this was pre-GPS), I set out on my own.

I headed to the address of the former orphanage and managed to find the place without getting lost and found a parking spot right in front. I turned the car off and just sat there staring up at the old redbrick structure. So this is where my life began, this is the place where my birth mother had walked out and left me, never to lay eyes on me again. I wondered how she had felt? Relieved? Sad?

With my purse in one hand and the information from

the State and my baptismal record in the other, I stepped out of the car and slowly started to walk up the concrete stairs to the main entrance on the left side of the massive building. I noticed that this section of the building was newer than the original and discovered that it was now the headquarters for the Dioceses of Albany.

I opened the large glass front door and stood in the lobby looking around like Dorothy the first time she set foot in Oz. I was amazed and a bit terrified that I was actually there. A few feet in front of me was an information desk. There were two older women standing behind the desk and one asked, "May I help you?"

I nervously approached and said, "I hope so, but it is rather a strange reason that I'm here."

I then proceeded to share my story. I told her I was born at Brady Maternity Hospital in 1953, at the time connected to the orphanage, and that I was placed here at St. Catherine's. I showed her the copy of my baptismal record. Reading the name of the priest who had baptized me, one woman said that she had actually known him. The women whispered something to each other, nodded their heads, then kindly asked me to wait where I was, that there was someone that I should speak with.

A phone call was made and within minutes a woman with short gray hair stepped off the elevator and approached me. She introduced herself as Karen* and asked me to take a walk with her. I hadn't a clue where we were going, but I willingly followed. We walked down a hallway just off the main foyer to an elevator. She explained that we were now in the original building that had been the orphanage.

We took the elevator up to the second floor. When the doors opened, we stepped out into another hallway. My guide turned right and the first thing I noticed was that all along the walls hung large old black-and-white

*name changed

66

photographs of children. She must have noticed me staring and told me the children were former residents of St. Catherine's. Was I in one of the pictures?

We walked into a dark room on the right that she explained had been the nursery, the room where I would have been. A chill suddenly ran through me like an electrical current. It was such a strange feeling to know that this was the room where I had spent the first part of my life. Maybe my crib would have been against the wall, or over by that metal-encased window. I just wanted to plop down on the old linoleum floor and spend a few minutes taking it all in. Oh, if these walls could talk.

She asked me to follow her down to her office so we could chat. As I walked out of the former nursery, I turned my head one last time to look around so that I would always remember what the room looked like, as well as what I envisioned it looked like in 1953.

We sat down in her office and the first thing she

asked was, "What are you looking for?"

I told her that I was looking for any additional information that the State hadn't shared with me. I knew that legally names could not be released, but there had to be something. I told her how much it would especially mean to me if I could find out if I had any siblings.

Without promising anything, she wrote down the name and address of a woman on a piece of paper and gave it to me. "Write to this person; she works in the archives. Explain who you are and what you are interested in. Share with her the information that the State gave you. Again, I cannot promise anything, but it certainly is worth a try."

I thanked her for her time and told her how grateful I was. I took the elevator down to the main lobby and said goodbye to the women at the front desk. I walked outside and got back into my car and, once again, sat there staring out the window at the old orphanage, thinking how glad I was that I had finally returned.

As soon as I arrived home from our trip to Connecticut, I sat down and wrote a letter to the person whose name I had been given in Albany. I explained that I had gone to St. Catherine's and was given her name in hopes that she could share additional information regarding my adoption. In as few words as possible I told my story. I did not hold out much hope that I would get a response or learn anything new, but I licked the envelope, put a stamp on it, and said a little prayer.

A couple of weeks later, on a warm summer morning in June, I went to retrieve the mail from the mailbox on the front porch. In between the bills and junk mail was an envelope with a return address from St. Catherine's.

I put all the other mail down on the kitchen counter and held the envelope. It felt thin, and I assumed that meant bad news: no news other than that the woman was very sorry, but there was nothing more she could share. I sat down at the kitchen table and opened the letter.

I was right; there were only a few paragraphs starting with "Dear Susan." But what I read in the second
paragraph would turn my world upside down, altering my
life from that moment on.

It said, "You have three half brothers, older than
you."

In that one instant, everything changed for me. "I
have three older brothers." I kept repeating it over and
over again. It was as though a beam of light was shining
down from above and illuminating those specific words.
Everything else on the page seemed blurred, everything
else seemed irrelevant. It did not matter at all that they
were half brothers. They were my brothers. This was the
information I had always hoped and prayed for—something I had always believed: I was not a "lonely child"
after all. This had be the missing part I had always felt,
the void that seemed to follow me throughout my life. I
couldn't believe that the State just omitted this informa-

tion, that they did not deem it important enough to tell me. I will never understand why they had not shared that with me years before.

I had sat my sons down a number of years ago when I thought they could understand and explained to them that I was adopted. I told them it was something that Nana and Papa never wanted to talk about but that they could always discuss it with me if they wanted. I remember at the time thinking to myself that I was asking them to keep a BIG SECRET just as my parents had done and continued to do.

So it was on that glorious morning that I bounded up the stairs two at a time with the letter in hand, crying and waking my still sleeping sons out of their sound sleep yelling, "Wake up! Wake up!"

As they each sat up in bed suddenly awakened and worried something terrible had happened, I told them in my breathless voice, "No, it's wonderful news, I have three brothers! You have three uncles!"

Of course this wonderful bit of news took several minutes to register with them. They were like, "Cool, Mom, but did you have to wake us up?"

I ran back downstairs to call Paul, friends, and anyone else I could think of, including my cousins in Boston. What an extraordinary moment in my life. I had brothers.

The letter stated that all four of us had the same mother, but only two of us had the same father. It wasn't clear who had the same father, but none of that mattered to me; they were my brothers no matter what.

I decided to call the phone number listed on the letterhead for Catholic Charities and I asked to be connected to someone in the archives. A woman answered and I told her the information I had just received. I asked her if there was anything she could tell me about my brothers: their ages at the time of my birth, anything. I wasn't asking for their names or anything identifying, but at least maybe I could figure out how old they were. She wasn't the friendliest-sounding person, she put me on hold, and when she returned on the line I could hear the shuffling of paper. I was thinking, she has all my information right in front of her, but she refused to tell me anything.

I asked her several questions. "Was my mother's name Susan or Ann? How old were my brothers?" By then I was crying, pleading and sounding more like a desperate child than an adult.

But there was nothing that she would share. She just coldly said that it would be illegal for her to tell me anything more than I already knew.

I hung up the phone feeling defeated and dejected. I just sat there staring off into space, trying to compose myself and thinking, "Okay, pull your self together."

I told one of my good friends, Robby, about the conversation and we came up with an elaborate scheme: We would drive to Albany, find the woman I had spoken to, one of us would distract her, and then the other would swipe my file and run. Of course we never had the courage to follow through with the plan, but it was nice to know that my friend would be happy to be an accomplice.

I had no idea how I was going to do it, but I was determined that somehow I was going to find my three brothers.

Certificate of Baptism

Chapel of the Maternity Hospital and Infant Home of Albany

30 North Main Avenue

Albany 5, New York 12205

The register of Baptisms in this Chapel attests that

Susan ████████

born in Albany, N. Y., the 12 day of October , 19 53

was baptized on the 23 day of October , 19 53

according to the Rite of the Roman Catholic Church.

Dated, this 22 day of .... 19 ....

....

CHAPLAIN

N. B. For canonical purposes, the Pastor should apply to the Chaplain for a full transcript of the record.

MY BAPTISAL RECORD

75

June 16, 1998

Susan E. Moyer

Dear Susan:

Your letters have been received, and I was able to locate your file through the use of your birth date.

In addition to the information you already have, I add the following:

> You were born at the Brady Hospital (as you know) on 10/12/53, and your weight was 8 lbs. 6 oz. (not 6 lbs. 8 oz. - seems trifling, but I thought you would be interested). You were 15 cm long and you were full-term. You had brown hair, blue eyes and a light complexion. You have three half-brothers, older than you. Only two of you have the same father. They were born during your mother's marriage.

> Your father was between 24 and 28 years old, was of Irish/German descent, Roman Catholic, finished high school and was a truck driver. There was nothing in our records regarding your mother's thoughts, other than that she felt it best for you to be adopted, as she was unable to care for you. You were discharged from Saint Catherine's on 4/23/54 to Albany Catholic Charities for placement in adoption. The rest is as you know it.

I have been in touch with Mary DeCotis and we determined that Saint Catherine's records had the most information. I hope the above is helpful to you. I wish there were more. This is actually more than I am able to obtain for most people.

It was lovely to be able to meet you, and I hope that some day the fact that you are registered with New York State Adoption Registry will bear fruit!

Most sincerely,

Administrative Assistant

LETTER STATING I HAVE THREE BROTHERS

ST. CATHERINE'S

BRADY MATERNITY HOSPITAL

TRUTH OR CONSEQUENCES

There was just one person with whom I had still not shared any of my exciting new information: my mother. My father had passed away a number of years ago. I made the decision that the discovery of my three brothers was so important to me, so monumental, that I had to tell her. But what would her reaction be? Would she become hysterical? Would she be angry? What if she stopped speaking to me? I had no idea what to expect, but it meant so much to me that I was willing to take the emotional risk.

A week after receiving the letter, I decided to visit my mother and share my news with her. Although my adoption was still an off-limits subject, I hoped she would say, "What wonderful news!" and share in my happiness. After all, no one else knew better how much I had wanted siblings, how much I detested being an only child, that "lonely child."

Driving the hour to my mother's apartment in Syracuse, I kept asking myself, *Am I sure I want to do this?* The anguish I felt was overpowering. I kept playing over in my mind the different scenarios that could come out of the conversation I was about to have. Maybe this wasn't the right thing to do. Maybe I should just let it go and let her continue to live in her state of denial.

Immediately after arriving, the two of us sat down at the kitchen table that is in front of the sliding door overlooking her patio and the woods behind. We started with a general conversation, as we always do, on how the boys were and what was new in our lives.

After twenty minutes, I decided it was now or never. *God,* I thought, *I wish Paul had come with me. How am I ever going to get through this? Am I doing the right thing in telling her?*

"Mom," I began cautiously, "I've received some wonderful news, news that means the world to me, and I would like to share it with you."

She looked at me, waiting to see what I would say next. I decided to let her read the letter from St. Catherine's herself. But before handing it to her, I said, "The information I'm sharing has nothing to do with how I feel about you or our relationship," trying to reassure both her and myself.

Feeling sick to my stomach, I handed her the letter and watched as she started to read. My eyes never left her face. I don't even think I blinked. I was looking for any reaction to what she was reading. There was none. Her facial expression did not change.

When she was finished reading, she simply folded the letter and slid it across the table to me and never said a word . . . not a damn word.

I said to her, "That's it? You don't have anything to say to me?"

She looked at me with a blank stare and immediately changed the subject. All I wanted to do at that moment was to get up and walk out of her apartment and get as far away from her as I could. Once again she chose to protect herself with total disregard to how I felt. Her reaction should not have come as any big surprise. But it hurt me in the most profound way.

Until the day she died, she never mentioned the letter or its contents.

She was my mother and should have rejoiced in what made me so happy. But looking back on that moment, I sense that she felt threatened. She wanted to protect herself from the information I had put in front of her, wanted to pretend that it didn't exist. And that is exactly what she did. She still chose to continue to keep her BIG SECRET and ignore the fact that I had found my biological brothers.

Although painfully saddened and disappointed by

my mother's response, I was more determined than ever to get back into searching for my brothers. I did some research and learned of a local adoptee support group and joined. When I went to my first meeting, I actually met individuals who were on the same journey as myself. I posted my adoption story on numerous websites for adoptees searching for their biological family members.

Adoptee Searching For Biological Family.
Born Susan Ann on October 12, 1953, at
Brady Maternity Hospital
Placed in St. Catherine's Infant Home
Mother - Irish/Canadian/Catholic
Lived Albany, New York
Three older brothers
Any information would be greatly appreciated

That was it. That was all the information I had, not very much to go on. Talk about searching for a needle in a haystack. And I was just one of thousands of individuals searching.

I then concentrated on the websites for adoptees in New York State, figuring I would be narrowing my search. I spent hours just reading other personal stories, all about people who wanted to know where they came from, just like me.

The summer of 1998 became a very important milestone in my adoption story. Knowing that I had three brothers out there somewhere made me feel not so all-alone.

HARD TIMES AND CHANGES
. . . WHY BOTHER?

In the spring of 2000, our family's world was turned upside down when Paul was diagnosed with cancer. We had noticed a lump on his neck, and after a battery of tests and a surgery, one cancerous spot was discovered on his left tonsil. He went through weeks of radiation, which rendered him weak and suffering an extreme amount of weight loss. Eating became quite difficult due to the radiation on his neck and throat.

That same year, Jeff was graduating from high school and heading off to college. That alone was traumatic for me. I would sit in his room at night and just cry after he left, especially with Paul so sick at the time. Our goal was for Paul to be able to sit down with the family and enjoy Thanksgiving—and thankfully he did. He is now eighteen years out and doing very well.

Periodically I would sit down at the computer and pick up where I had left off in my search to see if I had any responses to the many postings I had made or just try to discover anything new. But there was nothing.

Three years later, in 2003, it was Jason's turn to graduate and head off to college. Between kids, sports, work, and illness, taking the time to work on my family search continued to take a back seat.

In the spring of 2005, I decided to pull out my adoption file and take a look at it again. I happened to notice the name of the attorney who had handled the adoption for my parents. I went online and found that his telephone number and address were still listed after all these years. He still lived in the same town, Gloversville, outside Albany where my parents had lived when they adopted me.

I decided to call him; what did I have to lose? Surprisingly, he answered the phone himself. I introduced myself and explained that he handled my adoption in

1955. Although he did not remember my case—it was fifty years ago—he was very gracious and told me my adoption records would be on file in Fulton County. I am not sure what I was expecting him to do for me, but at least I was taking steps and starting back on my journey of search.

The following day, I wrote him a letter thanking him for his time and again outlined my story. He called me after receiving the letter and said he was touched by what I had written. He told me that he had gone to the courthouse and looked up my file. Although he was very kind and seemingly interested, nothing ever came of it. He never shared what he had found, but legally I guess he couldn't.

In March, something interesting arrived in the mail that would bring my search back to the forefront: an envelope with a return address from the New York State Adoption Registry. I recalled that at one of the adoption support group meetings I had attended, it was mentioned that the State was opening up a sibling registry. It would be similar to the one I had first registered with, but this one was just for individuals looking for their biological siblings, not their parents.

I read the letter, which explained how the sibling registry worked. All I had to do was fill out the form that was attached, mail it back, and if by chance one of my siblings were registered, the State would release their name and information. What were the chances that one of my brothers would be registered? Probably slim to none.

After mulling it over, I decided that although another avenue had opened, I would ignore the letter and not reply. Why bother when it was not even the State that had informed me in the first place that I had three brothers? Why would the State now divulge the information I was so desperately seeking? I doubted that any of my brothers even knew that I existed and it would just be a waste of time. I really wasn't up for hearing back from the

State telling me that I didn't have any siblings registered. I wasn't up for the hurt or feeling dejected. I had convinced myself that I would never find them. The story of my life's beginning would have no end. Sadly, that was just the way it was going to be . . . or so I thought.

I took the letter and form and buried it in my adoption file, and there it would remain . . . for at least a little while.

2005: THE YEAR
OF DISCOVERY

Several months later, on a beautiful Saturday evening in August of 2005, Paul and I were sitting outside our summer place drinking margaritas, relaxing and enjoying ourselves with the neighbors after a day at the beach. A new neighbor, a young woman, had joined our group and the conversation had turned to her. She began telling us that she was adopted and had recently found her birth mother and brother.

Wow, I thought, here was a topic close to my heart.

Unlike myself, she had known all of her life that she was adopted. She had searched and was lucky enough to have quite a bit of information, including names, which made finding her birth family pretty easy. I listened to her story, not revealing my personal connection to what I was hearing. I noticed Paul kept glancing at me as we listened. There were still a few people at the lake who knew my mother, and I was always careful to whom I told my adoption story, always vigilant of anything getting back to my mother.

The sun had set by now but no one had moved. We were still sitting around the picnic table, now lit by candlelight, enjoying the warm breezes off the lake. After a few more margaritas and after carefully scanning my audience, I decided to tell the story of my adoption. The ones who didn't know were intrigued and somewhat amazed that I had never shared that part of my life. The young woman who had been adopted told me that I had to keep pursuing and not give up on my search. I mentioned that five months ago, I had received the Adoption Registry information from the State but had just filed it away. She encouraged me to send the paperwork in. The evening's conversation once again had me thinking seriously about trying to find my biological family.

Back home on Monday morning, I started rummaging through my adoption files and dug out the information regarding the Sibling Adoption Registry. I decided to take her advice and filled out the form. As I stood over the printer making a copy for myself, I was thinking that even if I did hear back from the State, they would probably say, "Sorry, but you have no siblings registered, no one is searching for you." Why was I setting myself up for more disappointment?

Several weeks later, on a Saturday morning in September, Paul and I were heading out to the lake to close our summer place for the season. Just as we were leaving, the mail arrived. While standing in the kitchen, I quickly thumbed through the pile when something caught my eye. There was an envelope addressed to me with a return address from the State of New York Adoption Registry.

I sat down, nervously opened it, and read it aloud to Paul. The letter informed me that I had a biological sibling registered with the State. Oh my God! Could this truly be? One of my brothers was searching for his siblings?

I started to cry. Without hesitation, Paul told me to fill out the new request immediately. More paperwork. The form needed to be notarized and we could stop at the bank for that and go directly to the post office on our way up to the lake.

We made several copies then jumped into the car and headed to the bank to find a notary. I ran into the bank and up to the first person behind the counter that was available. The poor woman could barely understand what I was saying to her as I waved the document. "This needs to be notarized right away," I said. "It is extremely important and life-changing."

I babbled an explanation of what I was handing to her. Fortunately, she was very nice, signed and stamped the form, and wished me good luck. Next stop, the post office.

I could barely contain my excitement. *Which one of my brothers is searching for his sibling?* I kept thinking about the months that had passed since I first received notice from the State regarding the Adoption Registry and had just filed it away. If it had not been for the conversation on adoption on that recent and wonderful summer evening with our neighbor, I probably would have never mailed the form.

All I could do now was sit back and wait. How long would it be before I heard back? I had no idea—and patience is definitely not one of my strong points.

Corning Tower   The Governor Nelson A. Rockefeller Empire State Plaza   Albany, New York 12237

Antonia C. Novello, M.D., M.P.H., Dr.P.H.
Commissioner

Dennis P. Whalen
Executive Deputy Commissioner

CONFIDENTIAL

March 2, 2005

SUSAN F MOYER

ROCHESTER NY

Dear Ms. Moyer.

The services of the Adoption Registry have been expanded to include a biological sibling registry. This enables the Adoption Registry to share current names and addresses among registered biological siblings who give their final consents. If you would like to participate in the biological sibling registry, please complete the enclosed registration form. The form must be signed and notarized. There is no fee to participate in the biological sibling registry.

Please let us know if you have any questions.

Sincerely,

Peter M. Carucci
Director

LETTER STATING THAT THERE IS A
NEW SIBLING REGISTRY

WHAT A BIRTHDAY!

Weeks were going by, and still nothing from the State. Every day I would run to the mailbox after work to see if anything had arrived. It was now October 2005. The long Columbus Day weekend and my birthday were just a few days away. I would be heading down to our apartment in New York City for a weekend of celebrating. Because I had not received anything from the State, and I would not be home for several days, I decided to call them. I needed to find out the status of my paperwork. I knew my chances were slim that someone would actually share information with me, but what the hell. I would give it a shot.

I called the number for the Director of the Adoption Registry. I explained to the woman who answered that I had been waiting to hear back from the State for several weeks and that I was going out of town and wanted to know how much longer before I heard back from them. I told her that I was getting really tired of running home every day after work and checking to see if anything had arrived in the mail. "The suspense is killing me!" I said. She actually chuckled, and after putting me on hold for what seemed like an eternity, she came back on the line and told me that it had been sent out the previous day.

Two days later, on Thursday afternoon, still nothing had arrived. I was now heading to the airport to catch a flight to New York. Our good friends Rich and Robby were joining us for the long holiday weekend and staying at our apartment in the city. It was also Robby's birthday and we spent our birthdays together every year. This was her big sixtieth so lots of celebrating was planned. My son Jeff was home for the weekend and I told him that I was expecting something extremely important to come in the mail. He was to call me immediately if a green notice was left in the mailbox stating that a registered letter had arrived because I needed him to go to the post office right away to pick up the letter.

I didn't hear from Jeff on Friday so I thought that nothing had come. But by Saturday morning, I thought that if what the woman from the State had told me was true, it must have come. Sitting around the apartment having our morning coffee with Rich and Robby, I kept calling Jeff's cell phone to no avail. My anxiety and frustration levels were rising. I didn't care that it was Saturday morning and he was still sleeping: "Answer the damn phone!" Paul also kept calling Jeff's cell phone, and finally, around 10:00, Paul finally got hold of him. Sounding half asleep, Jeff said yes, a registered letter notification had been left in the mailbox the day before.

When Paul repeated this out loud, I grabbed the phone from him and told Jeff that he had to get up and go to the post office right away.

"All right!" he grumbled.

Paul warned me that because it was a registered letter addressed to me, Jeff might not be able to sign for it.

"Like hell," I said. I called Jeff back and told him that if anyone at the post office gave him a hard time, to call me, and let me speak with them to explain the situation. I hung up and began pacing the floor, unable to sit still waiting to hear back from Jeff. In fact, none of us could sit still.

After forty-five very long minutes, Jeff called back while sitting in his car in front of the post office and said, "I have the letter." I took a deep breath and told him to open it and slowly read the letter to me. My pulse rate was escalating. I clearly heard paper tearing as Jeff opened the envelope.

"Hurry up!" I impatiently shouted.

I was intently listening to each and every word, as he began to read.

Dear Ms. Moyer,

The New York State Department of Health Adoption and Medical Information Registry received all the notarized consents necessary to release identifying information (current names and addresses) regarding your registration.

Therefore, I am pleased to provide you with the following information:

Adoptee/Biological Sibling:
Richard A. Missita, (street address), Queensbury, New York.

The New York State Department of Health Adoption and Medical Information Registry appreciates the opportunity of serving you.

Best Wishes for a successful reunion.

"Oh my God!" I said. "That is your uncle, that is my brother!"

They didn't list a telephone number, but Paul was already on the computer looking up the address and phone number. I thanked Jeff, told him I loved him, and hung up.

Paul, Rich, Robby, and I all sat there with tears streaming down our faces. Paul not only found the number, he also looked up the address on Google Earth.

The picture on the monitor came into focus and I could not believe that I was actually looking at my brother's house. I'd found a brother, and his name was Richard.

Paul said that I should call him right away, but believe it or not, I wasn't ready. After all that I had been through, after all the years of praying for this, I really needed a few minutes to compose myself. I had been living fifty-three years without a sibling and now I had a brother with a name and I was actually going to speak with him.

I turned to Paul and asked, "Where the hell is Queensbury, New York?"

Paul said, "By Lake George. You've been there."

Borderline hyperventilating, I excused myself and went into our bedroom, closed the door, and sat down on the bed shaking and crying. It was all- so overwhelming. There were a couple of people I needed to call before I called Richard. The first was my son Jason to tell him the news. I then called a few close friends, but after that it was time to call my cousin Pat.

Pat was the one person who had been with me since I was that young girl questioning who I was and sharing my strong feelings that I was adopted. I wanted to tell her that I was no longer that "lonely child." Pat had been kept up to date on my search and knew I had been expecting to hear back from the State. I told her my big news and she was so thrilled that she cried right along with me. Sadly, the one person that I could not call—the only person who would not want to hear about any of this—was my mother.

About twenty minutes later, I felt that I was ready and a little more composed. I went into the bathroom and threw some cold water on my face, then walked back into the living room where everyone was waiting for me.

Paul asked me if I wanted him to initiate the phone call to my brother.

"Yes," I said. "Go ahead, I'm ready."

He went into the kitchen to use the landline instead of a cell phone. I heard him dialing the number and heard him ask, "Is this Richard Missita? Hi! My name is Paul Moyer and I believe that you are my wife's brother."

I held my breath listening for what was said next, but it seems that Paul was doing the listening. *What on Earth is my brother saying to him?*

It turns out that what my brother told Paul was pretty amazing. It seems that Jeff, in all his apparent nonchalant coolness about the whole thing, was actually pretty excited. After he had hung up with me, he called directory assistance to get Richard's phone number—while still sitting in his car at the post office. Jeff placed a call, introduced himself as Jeffrey Moyer, and said, "I believe that you are my mother's brother."

Then I heard Paul ask, "Would you like to speak with your sister?"

He handed me the phone. Trembling, and barely able to hold the receiver, I said, "Hello."

And then, for the very first time, I heard my brother's voice.

"Hello."

"I have no idea what to say," I timidly responded.

He said, "I have no idea what to say either."

Then he told me he had received the letter from the State the day before and had looked up my telephone number and left a message at our home. I explained that we were at our apartment in New York City for the week-end. This amazing conversation, with neither one of us knowing what to say at first, lasted for almost two hours.

I asked him if he preferred being called Richard, Rick, or Dick? He said Rick. I found out we are just seventeen months apart in age. He is married and has three daughters: the two older girls are his stepdaughters, the youngest, Andrea, his biological daughter, is just six months older than Jeff. He and his wife, Colette, had been married as long as Paul and I.

I just had to ask: "How tall are you?"

"Six foot," he said.

My brother was tall like me, tall like my sons, who are both over six feet. Tall—the very thing I wanted to change about myself growing up.

Richard had been looking for his biological family for fewer than two years. The reason for his delay in searching was that his adopted parents, both deceased, had never told him he was adopted. His parents had passed away two years ago, and Rick started looking for his birth certificate to get a passport. When he finally found it, he was shocked and confused by what he read. It was an amended birth certificate just like mine and said that he was born in Albany, New York. He was always told that he was born in Glens Falls.

He was soon to discover, at age fifty, that he was adopted. I thought being told at the age of sixteen wasn't right, but Rick's parents went to their graves with that secret.

Rick was new to this whole searching process to which I had devoted so many years. He had lucked out big time in starting his search with the resources that now were available. Rick's Non-Identifying paperwork stated that he had two older siblings but did not state if they were male or female. Now why did his Non-Identifying information from the State share that he had older siblings and mine did not? Of course there was no mention of a younger sister, for I was after the fact. Rick had assumed that I would be one of his older siblings. I told Rick about my years of searching and what information I had found along the way: that our older siblings were brothers and how I had discovered that in 1998. We now knew that our birth mother had given us both up for adoption. With us just being seventeen months apart, that would have meant that when she was pregnant with me she would have been signing the adoption papers for Rick.

We talked about our lives and families and shared what information the State had given each of us. I told him that our birth mother was one hundred percent Irish. I think this was a shock for him, for he was raised Italian and thought he looked Italian.

Richard, like me, was raised an only child. Although he had family members who knew he was adopted, no one ever said a word. But an aunt of his told him an interesting story after he discovered that he was adopted. She remembered his mother telling her about a phone call that she received from a woman asking if she would like a baby girl. Could that woman have been our birth mother who was trying to keep us together and find a home for me? Or could it have been someone else who had assisted in or had knowledge of Rick's adoption?

I actually found this thought to be comforting, that she at least had tried to keep us together. This meant there had to be some kind of connection between our mother and his adopted mother. Of course, no one will ever know what that connection might have been. Rick's adoption was different from mine, for his was private and happened right after he was born. Interestingly, he too was born at Brady Maternity Hospital, but he was never placed in St. Catherine's. His adopted mother not only had never told Rick that he was adopted and born in Albany, but she also had told some elaborate stories about his birth. Apparently she had had a hysterectomy prior to Rick's birth. Oh the stories and lies that are told.

Of all the information we shared that fateful Saturday morning, there was one bit of information Richard had that completely floored me. He said, "I know our mother's name."

What? How?

And then he said it: "Margaret Lillian Taggart."

I repeated it. "Margaret Lillian Taggart."

Oh my God. For the first time in my life I heard my mother's name, the name that had eluded me for fifty years. Rick said he learned her name from someone who was able to access his records. My emotions were at an all-time high. Here I was speaking to my brother on the phone and now I knew my birth mother's name.

The whole time I was on the phone, I was furiously writing down everything Rick told me on little pieces of paper that Paul would grab and take to the living room to share with Rich and Robby. When I wrote down that my mother's name was Margaret Lillian Taggart, Paul just looked at me. I actually still have the bits of paper.

Rick and I decided that we both needed to hang up and process everything. We were definitely on information overload. I said to him that we had a wedding to attend in Albany in two weeks and asked if he would like to meet.

"Of course," he said. So we made plans to talk again in the next couple of days.

After I hung up the phone, I went into the living room and collapsed into a chair. I shared what I had learned with everyone. Paul said he didn't think it was right to wait two weeks for Rick and I to meet. "How about we cancel your flight home and on Monday we take a train from Penn Station up to Albany with Rich and Robby?"

What a birthday present that would be.

Paul called Rick back right away and asked him, "Do you want to meet your sister on Monday?"

"Sure!" he answered.

So Paul arranged everything and I made a few more phone calls, then the four of us headed out the door to the nearest pub for lunch and a couple of drinks to celebrate.

I was feeling bad for Robby. It was her sixtieth birthday and everything that was happening overshadowed her celebration. But, like the wonderful friend she is, she said this was the best present she could have received and was thrilled to be a part of it.

As we celebrated throughout the city, including dinner at Scalinatella, I felt like I was two feet off the ground. I was as emotionally high as I'd ever been. The weekend flew by and before I knew it, it was Monday morning—time to catch a train to Albany to meet my brother. What a day it was going to be. I didn't get much sleep, and as we lay in bed in the early hours, I told Paul I didn't think I could do it.

"Do what?" he asked.

"Meet Rick."

That just didn't make sense at all, for what else had I hoped and prayed for all these years but to meet one of my brothers? But it was emotionally all too much for me. I felt sick with anticipation, but with Paul's encouragement, I decided I had to go. This was going to be one of the most important days of my life.

 **STATE OF NEW YORK**
DEPARTMENT OF HEALTH

Corning Tower   The Governor Nelson A. Rockefeller Empire State Plaza   Albany, New York 12237

Antonia C. Novello, M.D., M.P.H., Dr. P.H.   Dennis P. Whalen
Commissioner   *Executive Deputy Commissioner*

September 8, 2005

SUSAN E MOYER

Registry #

Dear Ms. Moyer:

A review of our records indicates that you have a biological sibling who was adopted. Your biological sibling is registered. If you wish to exchange your current name and address with your biological sibling, please complete the enclosed final consent form. Please note that identifying information will not be exchanged unless both you and your biological sibling submit your final consents.

The Adoption Registry thanks you for registering, and we hope to hear from you very soon.

Sincerely,

Peter M. Carucci
Director

BIOLOGICAL SIBLING REGISTRY LETTER

New York State Department of Health
Vital Records Section
P.O. Box 2602
Albany , NY 12220-2602

7001 1940 0007 5303 4783

02 1A $ 04.42
0004333468   OCT 05 2005
MAILED FROM ZIP CODE 12287

CERTIFIED MAIL
RETURN RECEIPT REQUESTED

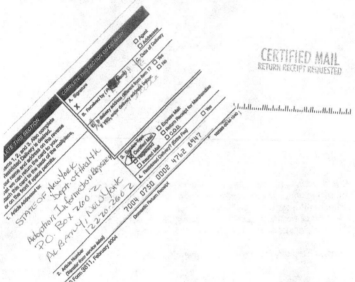

STATE OF New York
Dept. of Health
Adoption Information Registry
P.O. Box 2602
ALBANY, New York
12220-2602

7004 0750 0002 4762 8547

CERTIFIED ENVELOPE FROM

NYS DEPARTMENT OF HEALTH

■■ ■ ■■ DEPARTMENT OF HEALTH

Corning Tower   The Governor Nelson A. Rockefeller Empire State Plaza   Albany, New York 12237

Antonia C. Novello, M.D., M.P.H., Dr.P.H.   Dennis P. Whalen
Commissioner   Executive Deputy Commissioner

CONFIDENTIAL

September 23, 2005

SUSAN E MOYER

Registry #

Dear Ms. Moyer:

The New York State Department of Health Adoption and Medical Information Registry has received all the notarized consents necessary to release identifying information (current names and addresses) regarding your registration. Therefore, I am pleased to provide you with the following information:

Adoptee/Biological Sibling: **Susan E. Moyer**

                                    Rochester, NY

Adoptee/Biological Sibling: **Richard A. Missita**

                                    Queensbury, NY

The New York State Department of Health Adoption and Medical Information Registry appreciates the opportunity of serving you. Best wishes for a successful reunion.

Sincerely,

Peter M. Carucci
Director

LETTER FROM NEW YORK STATE TELLING ME

ABOUT MY BROTHER, RICHARD.

FACE TO FACE,
FLESH AND BLOOD

The four of us arrived at Penn Station early in the morning and boarded the train for the two-and-a-half hour trip up the Hudson to Albany. The ride up the river is very picturesque, but my mind wasn't on the scenery—instead it was on what would happen when we reached Albany. Paul, Rich, and Robby tried to distract me, but as the train drew nearer to our destination, I was feeling truly ill. Robby was checking my makeup and feeding me breath mints, trying to calm me down.

Then the train came to a stop. We had arrived.

Okay, I thought, *this is really it.*

Rich and Robby were staying on the train, for sadly they had to get back home to Rochester. I was so nervous, so anxious. All I wanted to do was to stay with them and keep going.

After tearful goodbyes, Paul and I stepped off the train. We were now on our own, and I hadn't a clue what was going to happen next.

I was walking along the platform dragging my heavy, oversized blue suitcase behind me when suddenly I stopped dead in my tracks. I glanced upward and found myself standing at the foot of what seemed to be the tallest and most endless set of stairs I'd ever encountered. *What, no elevator? Are you kidding me?*

But before I could look around for an elevator, Paul was already ahead of me, walking up the stairs two at a time, telling me to get going. Paul was carrying my garment bag and a bouquet of flowers that he brought to give to his new sister-in-law. I was already perspiring like I had just run a marathon.

I really had to make it to the top with my fifty-pound suitcase? Apparently, so up I trudged, thinking all the way that I would never make it without having a heart attack

When I finally reached the last step, I stopped and looked around. There were people standing everywhere, and to make it worse, all eyes seemed to be focused on me. Here I was in my moment of glory, going to meet my brother for the very first time, and I was panting like a dog and my makeup was starting to run from perspiration. Oh well, so much for making a great first impression.

I couldn't tell if these people were waiting to catch a train, waiting for someone else to arrive, or waiting to greet us. My eyes scanned the crowd and I tried to focus and find one familiar face. My handsome son Jeff had told me that he planned on driving to Albany for this very special moment, which meant so much to me. Then I spotted him through the sea of faces standing in the background holding a video camera, which was pointed directly at me saying, "That's her in the blue!"

I felt my knees buckling.

Suddenly, through an opening in the crowd, a man

started to walk directly toward me. As he approached, I noticed that he was several inches taller than I am, with brown hair, a mustache, glasses, and a warm smile. The next thing I knew, this perfect stranger put his arms around me in a big bear hug. I timidly put my arms around him and hugged him back. I wasn't sure how I was suppose to feel, and wasn't even sure I was feeling anything other than numb from head to toe.

After several moments we stepped back to take a good look at each other. So this is the person I'd been hoping to meet for so long, and now here he was standing right in front of me. This is my brother.

Rick introduced me to his wife, Colette, his two daughters Andrea and Therese, his son-in-law Jason, and his grandson Ryan. I introduced Paul, who handed Colette the flowers and hugged my brother. All of us had tears in our eyes—even some of the strangers who just happened to be standing there. To say it was a surreal moment does not do it justice. Words cannot describe what it is like to meet your brother as an adult for the first time.

Everyone had already met Jeff while waiting for our train to arrive. I had told Rick on the phone that Jeff was planning on being there, and he asked what Jeff looked like. Going on my description, Colette had seen a tall young man, whom she thought was Jeff, walking around the station and said to Rick, "I think that is your nephew." Rick was too nervous, so Colette walked up to Jeff and asked, "Are you Jeffrey Moyer?" When he said yes, Colette pointed over to where Rick was anxiously standing and said, "That is your Uncle Rick."

I am not sure how long we stood in the train station, but we decided to find a place where we could sit down and talk. We ended up at a nearby restaurant where they gave us a private room after Colette told the hostess our story. I sat next to Rick at a long table. It seemed that everyone was talking at once and staring, trying to see any resemblance.

I remember looking down at his hands that were resting on the table. I am not sure why I became fixated on them, but I was thinking that his hands carried the same blood that ran through my veins. He was the first person in my life, other than my sons, that I could say that about.

I looked across the table at my niece Andrea sitting next to her newfound cousin Jeff and thought how incredibly wonderful it was. I was disappointed that Jason was not with us, but he was at school and couldn't get away.

We all ordered something to eat and drink. Then after a couple of hours, it was time to say goodbye. Paul had to catch a train back to Manhattan and I was heading west on the thruway with Jeff for the three-hour ride home. We made plans for Paul and I to see Rick and Colette in Albany in a couple of weeks when we returned for the wedding.

The next day, Tuesday, I called my boss and told her

of all the events of the past few days and added that I would be coming into work a little late that day, as I was recovering from the previous day and the long trip home. When I arrived, my co-workers had gotten a cake and balloons to celebrate both my birthday and finding my brother.

When I returned home later that day, a beautiful floral piece had been delivered with a card signed, "Love, Your Brother Rick." Shortly after, my mother called me to wish me a happy birthday and see how my weekend in the city was. What could I possibly say? It was the best birthday I ever had and I met my brother. No, I could not share with her anything about the past four days of my life. After speaking with my family, including my cousin Pat, we agreed that at this point in her life, at eighty-eight, it was best not to upset her.

There were many telephone calls and emails between Rick and myself. I remember one time Rick called and Paul answered the phone and shouted, "Susan, your brother is on the phone." That was pretty strange, yet so wonderful to hear.

The four of us met again in Albany two weeks after our initial meeting. Rick and I shared stories about our lives. I told him more about the twenty-plus-year odyssey I had been on, and we compared the paperwork we each had regarding our adoptions.

I was ecstatic about the recent events in my life: finding and meeting my brother, learning my birth mother's name, all of it. But at the same time, there was a constant nagging feeling in my head that just wouldn't stop, and it was really bothering me. I wondered: Was it possible the State had made a mistake? What if Richard really wasn't my brother? I just needed to have some sort of confirmation before any more time passed and I became more emotionally attached. Maybe it just seemed too good to be true, that after all these years something had finally worked out for me.

Without sharing what I was feeling with anyone, the following week I placed a call to the Director of the NYS Adoption Registry. I spoke to him directly and explained that Rick and I had recently met through the Sibling Adoption Registry. I told him my concerns and asked how the State goes about proving one hundred percent that it is a match when they connect family members. I was put on hold so that he could retrieve my records. When he returned, he said that the State does multiple checks and confirms all the information one hundred percent before anyone is notified of a match. Rick and I were both directly connected to our birth mother; we definitely were brother and sister.

I called Rick right after and told him what I had been feeling and about the phone call I had placed to the State. Rick was glad I had called, for there was a little part of him that was worried too.

Weeks after Rick and I met each other, Paul and I went back up to our summer place. I wanted to tell the young woman who had told her adoption story that fateful summer evening what had happened in my life since then. I wanted to thank her for encouraging me to send in the sibling registration form. If it hadn't been for her sharing her story and prompting me to mail in the sibling registry, I probably wouldn't have done it and never would have met my brother.

When I was telling her about Rick and where he lived, her eyes grew wide and she told me that her birth father lived in the same town as Rick—Queensbury, New York. I called Rick and gave him her father's name and he actually knew him. It is such a small world—one that I would discover is even smaller than I thought.

RELATIVES AND RECORDS

My brother has an interesting story regarding his daughter Andrea and how the secrecy of adoption touched her life. Andrea had met a young man at work named Tony and a relationship started to form. Tony had the same last name, Missita, but as far as she knew, they weren't related. Andrea asked her father and it turned out that yes, Tony was a cousin, so Andrea had to end the relationship.

Right around the same time, Rick discovered he was adopted. This meant that there was no blood relationship between Andrea and Tony. The timing of Rick discovering that he was adopted changed not only his life but also his daughter's. Andrea and Tony were married in the fall of 2009. Paul and I attended the wedding. I sat there looking up at Andrea and Tony thinking that this day would never have been possible if it were not for the turn of events that had taken place. When the priest announced the same last name for the bride and groom—"Will thou, Andrea Missita, take thee, Tony Missita, to be your lawful wedded husband?"—those in attendance giggled. The priest looked up smiling, shaking his head, and said, "It's a long story."

Recently there have been stories on the national news about individuals finding and meeting their long-lost relatives for the first time. There are television programs dedicated to adoptees and shows about people's heritages and family roots. Many stories have some very strange twists. Some are of people who knew their family members but just didn't know that they were related. They grew up together, worked together, and in some circumstances romantic relationships such as Andrea's developed with the couples not knowing they were blood related.

In my opinion, this is just one more reason that adoptees' records should be unsealed. Many states are trying to pass bills that do just that—make everyone's records available. These bills would allow adult adoptees to obtain their original birth certificates and medical histories. There are a number of states where versions of this bill have already passed, but New York State is currently not one of them. The argument on the opposing side is that when the birth parent(s) put their child up for adoption, it is with the understanding that their information would never be released to the child.

I, of course, am coming from the point of view of the adoptee and strongly believe that it is the birthright of every individual that they have access to their records. Adoptees are the one group of United States citizens whose identities are withheld from them. The bureaucratic red tape, and arguments from people who are not adoptees block us from what is rightfully ours.

UPS AND DOWNS

The holidays were fast approaching and the end of what turned out to be a landmark year in my life was coming to an end. Jason had yet to meet his new uncle and family, so we decided to make plans to all get together. We chose the Turning Stone Casino located just outside of Utica, which is located almost halfway between my home and Rick's. We picked a weekend and booked four connecting rooms. Paul, myself, Jason, Jeff and his friend came. Rick, Colette, Andrea, Tony, Rick's daughter Therese, and her husband and sons also joined us. It was wonderful being together.

The year 2006 brought many wonderful events and one that was not so wonderful. The weekend of February 25, Rick and Colette came to our home in Rochester to spend the weekend. For me, it was another milestone—

Rich and Robby finally got to meet them. My children, stepchildren, grandchildren, and brother-in-law and sister-in-law all came over for breakfast so that everyone could finally meet my long-lost brother.

In June, our family went to Ireland for two weeks. The trip was a Christmas present from Paul. I had always wanted to visit Ireland. It is the land of my ancestors, although at the time I had no idea what part of the country they came from.

We rented a van and drove from one side of the beautiful Emerald Isle to the other. It was wonderful having our sons along for this experience. We took in a lot of sightseeing, and of course a few pubs. It was a fabulous and memorable trip. I wish that I had known my family history while on our trip and had been able to visit the places where my ancestors had lived; maybe I did. I felt such a strong kinship to the beautiful land and to the people of Ireland.

In August, Paul and I made our first trip to my brother's house. I was actually feeling nervous about going and kept saying to myself, I am spending the weekend at my brother's! It was still so alien to me that I had a brother I could visit. It was wonderful and we got to spend time with my nieces and their families, getting to know everyone.

I had been having a marvelous summer, which was flying by, and before I knew it September was upon us. On a Thursday afternoon, I went for my yearly mammogram appointment. I vividly remember the young technician intently studying the image she had just taken. I did not like the look on her face.

"There is a small spot that needs to be checked out," she said.

"Spot! What spot?"

The doctor looked at the images and told me that she was pretty sure that it was an early form of breast cancer, but again, she would not know for sure until a biopsy was performed. I called Paul in New York City and told him what was going on and he immediately told the boys.

A week later I returned to the Elizabeth Wende Breast Care clinic for a biopsy. Robby came with me for support. We both sat in the waiting room nervously chatting away like we always do. When my name was called, Robby gave me a hug and I followed the nurse into the examining room, still in disbelief that I was about to have a biopsy for cancer. When the procedure was over, I was sent home to wait for the results.

It was agonizing waiting to hear from the doctor the next day. Jeff called from Syracuse to see how I was doing. In the middle of our conversation I heard the garage door open. I went to see who it was and, much to my surprise, it was Jeff. He hadn't told me he was coming home to be with me. What a wonderful surprise.

Jeff and Paul were sitting with me when the call came

in. The diagnosis: stage one breast cancer. The doctor told me that it was very small, detected early, operable, and curable with surgery then radiation. She said that if you are going to get breast cancer, this was the one to get. I guess that was supposed to make me feel better?

The "C word." Cancer, is a terrifying diagnosis for anyone.

I told Jeff and Paul what the doctor had said.

The wheels were quickly put into motion, with doctor appointments including a surgeon, oncologist, and radiologist. It is amazing how many doctors one can obtain in a short period of time. It definitely takes a team to get someone through the necessary steps to recovery and remission.

I had a co-worker who had been diagnosed with the exact same cancer two years prior. She was a wealth of information and became my cancer buddy throughout the ordeal. I am so thankful that I had her help and that she knew exactly what I was going through.

The surgery was scheduled for October 11, 2006, the day before my birthday. Quite a different birthday from the previous year when I had met Rick. The day before my surgery, I spoke to Rick and told him that I would be fine and needed to get up very early the next morning. I was having a wire inserted in my breast prior to surgery to mark the cancerous site. I woke up at four-thirty the next morning to take a shower when Paul heard the doorbell ring. Who on earth would be ringing the doorbell at that hour of the morning? Paul opened the door and there stood my brother Rick. He had made the four-hour trip the night before and stayed at a local hotel. I was so surprised and touched but at the same time felt a bit uncomfortable; after all, my brother was still like a stranger to me. This was still so new to me, but I thought to myself, *So this is what brothers do—they're there for you.*

The surgery went well. Rick, Paul, Jeff, and my friend

from Syracuse were there. My lymph nodes and margins were clean, which was good news. I was very lucky that it ended up being the one little spot and was able to go home the same day. Rick was going to stay at our house that night instead of going back to the hotel. I healed well from the surgery and enjoyed Thanksgiving with my family. On November 29, 2006, I started my first of thirty radiation treatments.

The only discomfort from the radiation is the burning of the skin; but mentally trying to deal with what I was going through was a whole different emotion. Each day, Monday through Friday, I would head off to the hospital for my treatments. I met a lot of people there, the same faces each day going through the same type of thing. When someone would finish with their treatments, sadly a new face would appear.

Because of the daily radiation treatments, my commuting to New York City had been curtailed. I asked my doctor if I could skip a Friday so that I could have a long weekend to get away. She told me I could and that the missed treatment would be added at the end. I was ecstatic that I could get back to the city. While there, my son Jason and his girlfriend had gotten tickets to Madison Square Garden to see Jimmy Buffet, which was a wonderful diversion. Christmas was a bit of a blur, but with the support of family and friends, I made it through.

The year 2006 had started on such a high note but ended with being diagnosed with breast cancer and going through treatment. It was definitely a year of the good and the bad; the ups and the downs.

January 12, 2007 was my last day of radiation treatment. I was now cancer free.

WARMER DAYS AND
FAMILY TREES

Spring had finally arrived, and I was feeling well after the emotional events of the winter. On a warm, sunny Sunday afternoon in May, I was sitting out on the patio when my next-door neighbor came over to see how I was doing. She knew that I had continued searching for my family while going through treatment and that I had been united with Rick.

"Have you discovered anything new?" she asked.

"No, nothing new," I replied.

"I have a website that you really should check out: Ancestry.com."

She went on to share with me what she had discovered about her own family and about all the information available including historical documents and original records.

Curious, I decided to check it out for myself. I started by typing in my birth mother's name, which appeared as being in the records, but before being able to review the records, I had to join Ancestry. So out came the credit card and off I went once again into the abyss on my journey of search. It is fascinating to look through actual documents from census records and actual birth, marriage, and death notices. I called Rick and told him about Ancestry, and he immediately signed up and joined me in searching. After all the years of being alone in trying to find my family, it was nice to have someone else get involved. Rick and I would spend hours on the phone together at night perched in front of our computers exploring and discussing what information we came across.

One evening the phone rang. It was Rick. In a very excited voice, he said, "I found Margaret's manifest when she immigrated to the United States from Canada in 1927. Get on the computer and look up her name under border crossings."

I did as he said and there it was: our mother's immigration record. In May 1927, at the age of four, she immigrated with her parents, Mary and Robert Taggart, from Toronto, Canada, through Buffalo, New York, with the destination as Queens, New York. We were then able to look up the 1930 Census records and actually found them—with an addition to the family, a son born in 1929 in New York and named Robert, like his father.

We ended up with quite a bit of information on the Taggart family going back generations in Ireland. We posted the information that we had regarding our mother on Ancestry's search site in hopes that someone would connect.

One day, as I was scanning the posts on Ancestry, I came across one of the most interesting items. Someone had written that they were looking for someone named Margaret Lillian Taggart. Was it possible that someone was looking for the same person? Or had information on Margaret?

I found a contact number and quickly emailed the person, whose name was Kate. I noticed that she lived in Canada. We exchanged telephone numbers.

The next day I went to the local Church of Jesus Christ of Latter-day Saints to see if someone could help me on researching. They were wonderful, but we didn't find anything new beyond the manifest that we already had. I decided to call Kate later that evening.

Kate was gracious when we spoke. She shared a lot of information about the Taggart family. It turned out that my grandfather and her grandfather were brothers. Kate had spent a lot of the time researching the Taggart family tree and emailed me what she had.

I called Rick and told him about the phone conversation with Kate.

I definitely had the research bug again. I decided

with all the time I spent in New York City and with the family connection to the area that I would set out to see what I could discover. There had to be an abundance of information hidden in the archives somewhere, I just wasn't sure where.

The New York Public Library seemed an obvious choice to begin. Jason's girlfriend volunteered to help me in researching, so we headed to the research center located in the beautiful old public library on Fifth Avenue, which was built in the early 1900s. We walked up the steps past Patience and Fortitude, the stone marble lions that guard the main entrance. This impressive old building houses many historical records for the five boroughs. We spent a day sitting in the massive dark-paneled catalog room, lit only by the green-shaded desk lamps and the glow from monitors perched on desks looking over hundreds of records on microfiche. Research is time-consuming and involves a lot of patience referencing and cross-referencing. All I had was the information from the 1930 Census and the manifest: my birth mother's name, her parents' names, and that they had lived in Queens and Brooklyn. We looked up families with the name Taggart located in Queens and Brooklyn. We didn't find any pertinent information, but made notes on what we did.

Later in the week, I took the subway alone to lower Manhattan to the Municipal Archives, located near City Hall. I was handed a pair of white gloves and began searching through all the old records that were available. There I sat in the bowels of New York City looking through volumes of original old directories trying to find anything. Talk about a needle in a haystack.

My next stop was the Vital Statistics Department to see if I could obtain a marriage record for Margaret. I remembered reading that it is important never to mention the words "adoptee" or "adoption" when researching one's biological family. I was never able to tell anyone that

I was adopted and trying to find my family. This seemed ridiculous. Even though it should be everyone's right to find out where they came from, I was, by necessity, on a secret, covert mission. It was better just to say that I was doing genealogical research on my family when asked why I wanted permission to look through the archives.

But again, with so little information, I was just guessing that the names I came across were actual members of my family. I was guessing the years that my brothers could have been born; I was guessing at everything. It was like throwing a dart and hoping it landed on something.

I sadly discovered that the 1930 Census was the last one published, and the 1940 Census would not be made public until 2012. This was because the government decided it would release census records based on people's average life span.

Great. It was 2007 and I would have to wait five more years for the 1940 census.

But I kept going. Most of what I found was just guess-work on my part. It was frustrating yet fascinating to search through the old ledgers that covered the five boroughs of New York. They were in delicate condition and had to be handled very carefully.

I spent a lot of time and work on the Taggart family tree. I made telephone calls to family members that lived in Canada, Buffalo, and even North Carolina. I tried to locate immigration records in Buffalo and Niagara Falls, only to find out that in January 1938 the Honeymoon Bridge over Niagara Falls had collapsed, taking with it the building that housed many of the records I was looking for.

That certainly was a bit of discouraging news. It certainly didn't seem like I was getting any closer to finding Margaret or my brothers.

THE FIELD TRIP

It was now March of 2008—the month that always seems to me to be the gloomiest and longest of the year. Rick and Colette drove to Manhattan to spend the weekend with us at our apartment. I was looking forward to seeing my brother and thought it would be a perfect opportunity to do a little exploring. We made plans to go over to Brooklyn to the last known address we had for our mother, the one from the 1930 Census. Paul reserved a car with a driver to take us on our field trip across the East River to see what we could find.

We woke up Saturday morning to a bright and sunny day with a chill in the air. We took the elevator down to the lobby, and at ten o'clock a large black SUV pulled up and the four of us climbed in. We explained to the nice young man, who would be our chauffer for the day, where we were going and why, then we set off on our adventure.

We arrived at the address, a non-descript apartment building. The four of us climbed out of the car and stood on the sidewalk looking around like we had just arrived in a foreign country. My mother's former address was a five-story light brick structure situated on a street corner. It was a strange feeling to be standing there with my brother, staring up at the building where our birth mother had lived as a young girl. There was a bakery located on the opposite corner from the apartment building and a Catholic church on the other. We wondered if this was the church our family had attended. We decided to walk over and check it out.

We entered the beautiful old church. It was not very large, and we were the only people in there. Each step we took seemed to eerily echo off the stone- walls. It turned out to be a Polish Catholic church so we had doubts that this would be where our Irish family went. I picked up a church bulletin with the contact information of the church office.

After leaving the church, the four of us piled back into the car and asked the driver to drive us around the neighborhood. Since we had no specific destination in mind, I cannot imagine what he must have thought of us. About a half an hour later, we told him that he could head back into Manhattan. I am sure he was relieved to do just that.

On Monday morning, I called the church to see if any of my family names came up under their baptismal, communion, or marriage records. Of course it was another dead end. There were no Taggart's affiliated with the church.

Although nothing came of our excursion to Brooklyn, it did give us a feeling of being a little closer to our birth mother, and of course, spending time together.

THE VERY SMALL WORLD

In April, Paul and I flew to Aruba for a much-needed vacation. One glorious hot day, we were hanging out and relaxing at our favorite bar, enjoying a few cocktails and a bite to eat. The bar sat on a pier over the clear turquoise waters of the Caribbean. Paul had excused himself to use the restroom when two couples approached the bar to order drinks. I noticed that one man wore a T-shirt with the name of a town on Cape Cod printed on the front. As he stood next to me waiting for his drink order, I asked if he was from the Cape.

"No," he answered, "I'm from New York State."

I told him that we were from New York State and asked what part of the state he was from.

He said, "Somewhere you probably never heard of located up north near Lake George—a town called

Queensbury."

I just stared at him for a moment, letting it register. *Is this some kind of joke? Now I know that it's a small world, but are you kidding?*

"Really? My brother lives in Queensbury!" I proudly exclaimed.

"What is your brother's name?" he asked.

"Rick Missita."

As soon as I said the name, an astounded and confused look appeared on the man's face. "Really? I know Rick Missita, I've known him for years. I never knew he had a sister!"

Before I could say another word, he called his wife and friends over and said, "This is Rick Missita's sister!"

They were all in disbelief. I briefly told them that Rick and I were adopted and had just found each other a couple of years ago. Paul walked back in and I told him that the four people standing there were from Queensbury and knew Rick. The same look that I had appeared on Paul's face—disbelief. What are the chances that while sitting in a bar in Aruba, I would have a random conversation with a total stranger, and he knows my brother?

As soon as we made it back to our room, I grabbed my phone and called Rick. When I heard him answer, I said, "You are not going to believe what just happened!"

Small world? You better believe it!

I FOUND HER! SHE'S DEAD,
BUT I FOUND HER!

One hot afternoon in late August, I received an email from my old friend Chris. She had just returned to her home in Florida after a visit to Rochester. Chris wrote that if I went online to Yahoo, I would see the pictures that she had posted from our evening together. I clicked on the Yahoo webpage and realized that I needed to be a member in order to view the pictures. I tried to set up a password but was informed that I already had one. I did? Then it dawned on me: back in January, I had registered with Yahoo's New York State Adoptees website, one of the numerous websites I had registered with over the years while searching for my biological family. I requested my long-forgotten password, clicked on the mailbox, and much to my amazement I was informed that I had over 7,000 pieces of mail.

Yikes, I thought, this should be interesting.

I began scanning through all the emails, deleting most and only reading the ones that could possibly pertain to my personal search. Because it had been months since I had written my post, I decided to repost my information.

Within days I received a number of responses, primarily from a woman who was known as a "search angel," an individual who helps people with their searches. Some of the information she sent I had already obtained, but on the afternoon of September 4, 2008, as I sat down to check my emails, there was another message from her.

It was just three years prior that I had learned my birth mother's name was Margaret Lillian Taggart, and that later the last name Costantino had been added, I presumed from someone that she had married. I also had the year of her birth as either 1923 or 1924 and that she was born in Toronto, Canada, had immigrated to Brooklyn, and was last known to be living in Albany, New York.

The email suggested that I look at the list of women's names she had gathered from obituaries found in the Albany newspapers. All of the listings started with the name Margaret and all were born in either 1923 or 1924. The last names varied, but because women change their names due to marriage, she said it might be worth a look. What did I have to lose? None of the last names were Taggart or Costantino, so I was certainly not feeling very optimistic, but I figured, what the heck.

There were twelve names on the list, and I came across the name Margaret L. O'Connor who had died on March 11, 1998. There were no other Margaret's with the middle initial L. The name appeared twice on the list, the only name to do so. For some inexplicable reason, I was drawn to this name. It was number six on the list, an Irish name. I decided to click on it.

An obituary appeared on the screen and I slowly started to read: Margaret L. O'Connor, 74, died on Wednesday,

March 11, 1998, in St. Peter's Hospital. Born in Toronto. Raised in Brooklyn, New York, and then moved to Albany where she remained.

Oh my God. Is this for real? Is this her?

With my heart beating faster, I continued to read. Survived by her sons Charles and John Costantino. My brothers? The obituary mentioned Margaret's brother, Robert, who I did know about from the 1930 Census, and a sister, Geraldine, who I did *not* know existed, as well as several nieces and nephews, grandchildren, and her good friend Mary David, and her daughters.

Holy crap!

It was as though I could hear angels singing the "Hallelujah Chorus." *For God's sake, I'm reading an obituary*, I thought. And yet, to me each word was so beautiful, it was as though an artist's fine-point sable brush had meticulously applied each word with vibrant colors. Finally, after all of the years of searching, I had the names of my oldest brothers: John and Charles.

I must have read the obituary five times.

Physically shaking, I ran to the telephone to call Rick. Of course he didn't answer. *Really? Damn. Where the heck are you? This is huge!* I left a message to call me as soon as possible and that it was very important. I then called Paul in New York and screamed into the phone, "I found her, I found my mother! She's dead, but I found her!" Of course he had no idea what I was talking about and thought I meant the mother that he knew, my adoptive mother.

"No!" I shouted, "it's my birth mother, and I have the names of my brothers!"

I was feeling excitement and total shock at that moment. Rick called me back about twenty minutes later and again I was yelling into the phone, "I found her, I found our mother, she's dead, but I found her!"

Have you looked in Albany county for divorce records?
How long ago & where did you look for marriage records (at the state
library, NYC, Rochester, Syracuse, or maybe Buffalo?) ??
I wonder if it would be worth my time to recheck them for you?
   Can you tell me if BOTH you & your brother have gotten Non-id, so
that you can narrow the 'window' of when she was born down.. and compare
those infos to the 4/11/1930(she was listed as 6) census & also the
5/30/1927(she was listed as 3, and born in Toronto, Ontario, Canada)
immigration record?
If your brother's record had Taggart crossed out & Constantino written
on.. it would appear that between his (1952? birth) and his 1953
adoption finalization that she must have remarried between those two dates.
Can you give me the specifics of the dates involved in both your births,
non-ids & his finalization?
I'm also trying to see if a friend can check Canadian birth records for
Margaret.
Thanks,
Kathy

Have you checked this women's obituaries to see if the name Taggart is
listed???

MARGARET MACDONALD   05 Jun 1923   Dec 1987   12206 (Albany, Albany, NY)
12206 (Albany)   New York

MARGARET KRAUSSE   26 Jun 1923   Feb 1993   12211 (Albany, Albany, NY)
(none)   New York

MARGARET T GALLUP   23 Nov 1923   14 Jun 2006
   12211 (Albany, Albany, NY)   12211 (Albany)   NY

MARGARET L OCONNOR   18 Dec 1923   11 Mar 1998
   12085 (Guilderland Center, Albany, NY)   (none)   NY

MARGARET ROHAN   20 Dec 1923   23 Apr 1998
   12185 (Watervliet, Albany, NY)   (none)   New York

MARGARET L OCONNOR   18 Dec 1923   11 Mar 1998
   12085 (Guilderland Center, Albany, NY)   (none)   NY

MARGARET ARGAY   07 Mar 1924   Feb 1989   12047 (Cohoes, Albany, NY
<http://resources.rootsweb.com/USA/NY/Albany>   (none specified)
               New York

MARGARET HUNT   15 Jan 1924   15 Apr 2008
   12110 (Latham, Albany, NY)   (none)   New York

MARGARET WOODS   05 Mar 1924   Dec 1987   12211 (Albany, Albany, NY)
(none)   New York

MARGARET ARGAY   07 Mar 1924   Feb 1989   12047 (Cohoes, Albany, NY)
(none)   New York

MARGARET MILLER   16 May 1924   25 Aug 2007
   12110 (Latham, Albany, NY)   (none)   New York

MARGARET ARGAY   07 Mar 1924   Feb 1989   12047 (Cohoes, Albany, NY
<http://resources.rootsweb.com/USA/NY/Albany>   (none specified)
               New York

OBITUARIES SENT TO ME TO LOOK AT NAMES

ALBANY -- **Margaret L. O'Connor**, 74, died Wednesday, March 11, 1998 in St. Peter's Hospital. Born in Toronto, Canada, she was raised in Brooklyn and then moved to Albany where she remained. Mrs. O'Connor worked for Albany International Felt Company for 32 years until her retirement. She was a communicant of St. James Church and a member of the Sheehy-Palmer V.F.W. Post 6776 Ladies Auxillary. Mother of Charles and John Costantino; sister of Robert Taggart and Jerry   , sister-in-law of Bob   ; aunt of Kathy   , Cindy   and Tim   . Also survived by four grandchildren, three nieces and three nephews; friend of Marion (Mary)   and her daughters. Funeral service Saturday at 8:15 a.m. from the McVeigh Funeral Home, 208 N. Allen Street, Albany thence to St. James Church at 9 a.m. where a Mass of Christian Burial will be celebrated. Relatives and friends are invited and may call Friday from 5 to 8 p.m. in the funeral home. Those wishing to remember Margaret in a special way, may send contributions to the Lupus Foundation or the St. Jude Children's Research Hospital. MCVEIGH FUNERAL HOME 208 N. Allen Street Albany, NY 12206 518/489-0188

MARGARET'S OBITUARY

FEARS, TEARS, AND
TELEPHONE CALLS

After speaking with Paul and Rick and calling my sons, friends, and anyone else I could think of, I went back on the computer and started looking up every name in the White Pages Directory for the Albany area that was mentioned in the obituary. I spent the entire evening calling the telephone numbers I thought could be possible matches, but as usual, I had no luck.

When I went to bed that night, for the first time in my life I was feeling hopeful that I just might be able to find my brothers. I kept saying the same thing over and over to myself: "I found her. I really found my birth mother." Maybe it's strange, but the fact that she had been dead for ten years didn't really bother me the way one might think. For many years, I was under the impression that she was no longer alive—it was just a feeling I had. The coincidence is that she died in 1998, the same year I discovered that I had three older brothers after my visit to St. Catherine's.

The next morning was Friday, September 5, and the start of the long Labor Day weekend. I was heading out of town up to our summer place later in the day, but I decided to spend a little more time researching before I left. Again I went back to the names in the obituary, thinking if I could find and connect with just one person I would be lucky. It is such a long and tedious process of matching locations, names, ages, and telephone numbers. I decided to search for Margaret's sister, listed as Geraldine Mayer* and married to a Robert Mayer*, living in a suburb of Albany. Well, at least they were there ten years ago in 1998.

And then ... bingo! I discovered that Geraldine and Robert Mayer were still living in the same town. Terrific, they were still around. There was no telephone number so

*names changed

I called directory assistance and asked for their number. Unlisted! Of course it was. Why would I be surprised? So now what? I then came across a Tim Mayer*, Geraldine and Robert's son, living in the same town as them. Could it be? I was going to find out.

Once again I called directory assistance and luckily his phone number wasn't unlisted. *Okay,* I thought, *I'm going to call him, here goes.* I didn't know what the hell I would say to him, but I was determined to go through with this

It was Friday afternoon; would anyone even be home? And how did one begin a conversation such as this? How could I come off not sounding like a deranged individual and have him hang up on me?

I took a deep breath and dialed the number. After several rings a man said, "Hello."

"Hi, is this Tim Mayer?" I nervously asked.

"Yes."

"Are your parents Geraldine and Robert Mayer?"

"Yes," he answered.

"Did you have an aunt named Margaret L. O'Connor?"

Again he answered, "Yes."

"Well, my name is Susan Moyer and what I am about to tell you could be a bit of a shock. I am Margaret's daughter who she gave up for adoption in 1953."

For what seemed like minutes but was only seconds, he paused then said, "Oh. I knew that Margaret had two sons, but did not know there were any other children."

"Actually there are two of us that she had put up for adoption; there was another son." Tim seemed to take all of this information in stride. I came to an uncomfortable question.

I asked him if his parents were still alive, and he said yes.

"Do you think that it would be okay if I call your mother?"

He said that he thought it would be fine, and gave me Geraldine's number. I thanked him for speaking with me and hung up the phone.

Well, that went pretty well, I thought. I then called Rick and filled him in on what I had been up to and my conversation with our cousin Tim. I also needed some encouragement before I would be able to make the next important phone call.

With shaking hands, I dialed Geraldine's number. I almost hung up when I heard a man answer the phone. "Hi, my name is Susan Moyer and I was wondering if it would be possible to speak with Geraldine?"

He said, "Yes, hold on a minute." I was so thankful that he had not asked me the reason for my call, for I felt that chances were that she might not have been willing to speak with me.

The next voice I heard was a woman asking, "Hello?"

"Hi, my name is Susan Moyer." I paused for a second to formulate just how to ask my first question. "Were your parents Robert and Mary Taggart?"

"Yes," she hesitantly answered.

"Was your sister Margaret O'Connor?"

Again she answered, "Yes."

What on Earth must she have been thinking at that moment?

"Well, this will come as quite a surprise, but I am Margaret's daughter that she gave up for adoption in 1953."

"Oh? I knew that Margaret had given up one child that I thought was a boy, but I never knew about a girl."

"There are two of us, myself and my brother, who she gave up for adoption. We are just seventeen months apart and we were both born at Brady Maternity Hospital in Albany."

"I don't know anything about that," she replied. I thought it strange that Geraldine lived near her sister and must have spent time with her but didn't know that Margaret was pregnant for two years.

"What is it that you want?" Geraldine asked, sounding somewhat annoyed.

"Just information about my birth mother, nothing else." I said. I was afraid that the conversation would come to an abrupt end before I could ask all my questions.

She told me that Margaret had gotten pregnant at age seventeen while living in Brooklyn and had gone to Maryland to marry the father of her child, Charles Costantino, This is something that I would later question upon obtaining Margaret and Charles's marriage certificate, which said they were married in a Catholic church in Brooklyn. Maybe they first had a civil ceremony in Maryland?

Geraldine went on to say that Margaret had her second son, John, three years later.

"Margaret's husband was very abusive, and she decided to leave him, but he would not let her take the children. Margaret packed up and left her husband and her sons and moved to Albany, where I was already living with an aunt after my mother had passed away. My father had left and moved back to Canada."

"What do you know about my brothers Charles and John? Did Margaret ever go back to Brooklyn for them?" I asked her.

"No, she was estranged from them. It wasn't until right before her death in 1998 that somehow they had tracked her down." She said they lived in Staten Island or somewhere near there.

"Do you have any pictures of my mother?" I asked.

"No," she responded. I found that to be quite odd. How could you not have pictures of your sister?

I asked her if she would describe Margaret, and she said that she was tall, fun, and a nice person.

Tall. Finally I knew where my height came from.

She did comment that Margaret did not have much luck with relationships.

Obviously, I thought.

What Geraldine told me next shocked me. She said that Margaret was only her half-sister. She explained that sometime in the 1970s, Geraldine, her family, Margaret, and their Aunt Beatrice from Toronto (or Aunt Bea, as everyone called her) went on vacation to Italy. It was while there that Aunt Bea announced to Margaret and the family that she was really Margaret's birth mother.

This Aunt Bea, Mary's sister, was really Margaret's biological mother? Mary was actually Margaret's adopted mother? How interesting that Margaret had put both Rick and I up for adoption, and now I'd come to find out our mother was an adoptee herself—which she didn't discover until late in her life!

Aunt Bea would travel from Toronto frequently to

spend a lot of time with Margaret and Geraldine. She had always been in their lives. That was all Geraldine would say regarding this interesting bit of information.

I then asked her about her brother, Robert Taggart, and she quickly said that no one had anything to do with him, although his name was mentioned in the obituary.

I asked who this O'Connor was. She said his first name was Donald and that he and Margaret were married for about nine years.

I could tell by the sound of Geraldine's voice that she was growing weary of the conversation. Again she asked me, "What do you want?"

Once again, I reassured her that all I wanted was information about Margaret, nothing else. Although I had a million more questions, I did not want to aggravate her. She did ask me for my telephone number and address, which I gave to her.

I thanked her for speaking with me then quickly

called Paul and Rick to relay what I had discovered from my telephone conversation with Geraldine. Then I just sat, trying to formulate everything that I had learned.

Suddenly, I looked up at the clock and realized how much time had passed. I needed to get going. I was stopping in Syracuse to take my mother out to dinner for her birthday before heading up to the lake. How on Earth was I going to go out to dinner with my mother and act normal with my head buzzing from all the events of the past forty-eight hours? I had no idea, but I knew it sure wasn't going to be easy.

As soon as I picked my mother up at her house and headed to the restaurant, she immediately asked me what was new.

"Oh, nothing much," I timidly replied. Are you kidding me? Everything was new! I didn't want to be rude, but dinner with my mother couldn't end fast enough. It was all I could do to keep my mind off all the new developments that had transpired earlier in the day. I took my mother back to her place as soon as dinner was over then I headed north to the lake.

First on my agenda was to have a cocktail on the deck with Paul while I filled him in on all the news. That whole weekend I was consumed with what I had discovered. I kept replaying my conversation with Geraldine and wondered what the hell was going to happen next. Where did I go from here?

A PILGRIMAGE TO ALBANY

The holiday weekend was over, and although I had a nice time, I was anxious to get back home and on the computer. I called Rick the following Tuesday morning. He was actually in his car driving to Albany. He had decided to help in the search, so with our mother's obituary in hand, he was heading off to see what he could come up with. His first stop was the funeral home that had handled our mother's funeral to see if they would share any information. They didn't have much to add, other than that it was Geraldine's daughter who made the funeral arrangements. Rick then headed to the cemetery where our mother was buried to find her grave. On the headstone is her name, her birth and death years, praying hands, and, below them, the words "Say a Hail Mary."

Leaving the cemetery, Rick then drove to the apartment building where Margaret had last lived. Listed in the obituary was a woman named Mary, a friend of Margaret's. Since the obituary was ten years old, we had no idea if this Mary was still alive or still lived at the same address.

Rick went into the office and spoke with a woman named Donna. Rick explained who he was and why he was there, trying to tell her our story in an abbreviated form. Donna had been working there for many years and in fact, remembered our mother. She said that Mary still lived there in the same apartment next door to the one our mother had lived.

After Rick finished telling her our crazy tale, Donna called upstairs and spoke with Mary. She told her that Margaret's son was standing in front of her and relayed everything Rick had just said. Understandably, Mary was quite shocked and also apprehensive. Who knew the last time she had even thought of Margaret? Mary said she needed some time to think and wouldn't come downstairs to meet Rick at that time. Rick thanked Donna for her time and left his telephone number to give to Mary. He called me from his car and filled me in on what he had discovered. He gave me Donna's phone number and I told him I would call later that afternoon to back up everything he had shared with her.

When I called Donna and explained to her who I was, she said that after Rick had left, Mary had come down to the office to be filled in on what he had talked about. Mary told Donna that Margaret had shared with her years ago that she did give a child up for adoption but never spoke of it again. I gave Donna my telephone number to give to Mary, saying that she could call Rick or me any time.

While still in Albany, Rick had tracked down an address in an old city directory and found where Margaret had been living in the 1950s, which was where she resided when she had given birth to both of us. He went to the location on McPherson Terrace.

The street was lined with old Brownstones or row houses. At one time it must have been a lovely neighborhood, but now the buildings were pretty dilapidated. Rick took pictures and emailed them to me. I stared at the pictures, fascinated that this was where our mother had lived, the place she returned to twice after giving birth and returned childless.

In the meantime, I sat down and wrote a letter to Geraldine, thanking her for speaking with me, and sent it by certified overnight mail; that way I could confirm that she received it. I included a picture of myself, asking her if she saw any resemblance to Margaret, and also added pictures of my sons, Margaret's grandchildren. Sadly, and much to my great disappointment, she never responded.

MEETING AN OLD
FAMILY FREIND

Two days later, Thursday, September 18, I called Donna and told her that Mary hadn't called Rick or me. "That is surprising," Donna said. "Mary told me that she was going to call you."

I told Donna that I was planning on driving to Albany the following Tuesday, September 23, to meet Rick and that we would love the opportunity to sit down with Mary. "It would mean the world to both of us."

"I'll call Mary right now to tell her you will be coming to Albany and will let you know what she says." All that was left for me now was to pray and keep my fingers crossed that Mary would agree to meet with us.

I didn't have to wait very long for an answer. Donna called me first thing the next morning to say, "Mary has agreed to meet with you and Rick."

"Thank you, thank you," was all I could say. I kept thinking that I was going to actually meet someone who knew my birth mother. Tuesday could not get here fast enough.

I called Rick and told him the good news. I also told him this was something just the two of us needed to do alone, without Paul and Colette. "I'll see you in Albany on Tuesday morning. We are going to meet Mary! Hallelujah!"

Tuesday, September 23, 2008, finally arrived. I was like a child on Christmas morning, waking up before dawn after a sleepless night. My adrenaline was pumping. I could not wait to get on the road and head east to Albany. I showered, had two cups of coffee, and was in my car by seven. The three-hour drive seemed endless. I had the radio on the oldies station the whole way, singing out loud just trying to pass the time.

The weather was perfect. I made it to Albany, met

Rick at our scheduled meeting place, and climbed into his car.

Our first stop was the cemetery where our mother is buried. What a strange feeling, standing over Margaret's grave. It was not sadness, but pure amazement that I felt. After all these years, I had finally come to this point in my journey. How strange it was to be reunited with my birth mother for the first time since she had given me up for adoption over fifty years ago.

At this point, we figured that Margaret must be rolling over in her grave with the two children who she gave up for adoption standing over her.

Surprise!

As I stared down at her grave, I silently asked, "Who are you?"

I thought of all the unanswered questions that were buried with her.

"Why?" There were a lot of whys.

After leaving the cemetery, Rick and I headed over to the funeral home. We sat down with one of the owners to see if there was anything new that would help us in finding our brothers. Again, we came up empty. We then drove over to our mother's former address at 5 McPherson Terrace. We parked the car directly in front of the old worn and neglected-looking row house and sat staring at the place. I discovered that these Brownstones are now on Albany's list of most endangered historically valuable buildings.

How surreal for Rick and I to be sitting in front of what was Margaret's home. That is the door she entered and exited through every day she lived here. And this is the place she lived when she was pregnant with both Rick and I, and the place where she returned without us.

After about twenty minutes, we headed over to St. Catherine's, the old orphanage. I had not been back since 1998. Again, we did not get out of the car, but just sat there looking up at the old building. It was different being here this time, for I was not alone. The last time I was here, I didn't know I had three brothers. I found it comforting to have Rick by my side. I had come a long way.

We noticed it was now a little after eleven and time to leave. Our next very important stop was meeting Mary.

We pulled into the parking lot of the multistory apartment complex. Rick and I looked at each other and said, "Here goes!" For the first time in our lives, we would be meeting someone who knew our mother.

We walked into the main entrance and Donna was at the reception desk to greet us. I had brought a bouquet of flowers to give to Donna to thank her for all her help in setting up this momentous meeting.

"Mary is in the community room waiting for you," she said.

We followed her down the hall and entered a large room where a woman sat alone. She stood to greet us.

Mary was a beautiful, warm, and spry eighty-four-year-old woman. After we both hugged her, we all sat down, Mary on my left and Rick on my right. Rick and I both had our own list of questions, neither written in any particular order for we really had no idea where to begin.

Fortunately, Mary started the conversation by telling us about her friendship with Margaret, which had started in the 1970s and lasted until Margaret's death. She told us how years ago, Margaret had told her that she had given up a son for adoption, but she never brought the subject up again. She never mentioned a daughter, although one of Mary's daughters thought she remembered a time when Margaret had mentioned giving birth to one.

The conversation then turned to my brothers, Charles and John. Mary said, "Margaret left their father, who was an abusive man, because she couldn't take it any longer, but in doing so, she left behind her two sons and never returned for them. Margaret had from time to time mentioned going back to Brooklyn for the boys, but she never did. Margaret had told me several times that she would never be a good mother."

This was a fair and interesting comment, considering that she had given birth to four children and abandoned them all. As a mother myself, I just could not for the life of me imagine giving up any child, let alone four.

What Mary said next stunned both Rick and me. "Your brothers spent many years searching for your mother," she told us. "They found her one month before she died."

I had to process what she had just said. So all the years that I had been searching for Margaret, they had too?

Mary went on to say that my brothers had hired a private investigator to help them in their search, and it was in February 1998 when the investigator called them with the news that he had located Margaret. It was the same year I discovered I had three brothers. What a strange coincidence.

At the time, Margaret had been living in a nursing home due to ill health. As soon as John and Charles had received the news of where Margaret was located, they headed to Albany. Mary happened to be at the nursing home when they arrived on that February day. It was the first time they saw her since she had walked out of their lives when they were three and six years old. In they walked, bearing flowers and balloons. They even had a mother's ring made for Margaret with their birthstones.

But when Margaret heard that "the boys"—as she referred to them—had found her, she refused to see them. Nonetheless, Charles finally had enough and walked straight into her room to confront her.

She said to him, "Do you remember what I said to you the last time I saw you?"

"Yes," he answered. "You would come back for us."

Are there any other children?" Charles asked Margaret.

"No," she answered.

A lie.

Geraldine arrived, and when she saw Charles and John, she asked Margaret, "Are you going to change your will now?" How heartbreaking for them. After all that time, after being abandoned by their mother and spending time and money trying to find her, that was the welcome they received. John had entered the room to see Margaret, but he was so upset by her and Geraldine's attitudes that he walked out, never to return. Before Charles headed out the door, he placed the ring he had brought on Margaret's finger. Margaret passed away one month later. John refused to go to the funeral. It was only Charles and his daughter who returned to Albany.

I asked Mary if she knew where my brothers lived.

"One is in New Jersey, and one is on Long Island."

Hmmm, not Staten Island as Geraldine had told me. Mary said that one of them owned a restaurant, she just wasn't sure which one. Mary told of all the fun and "hell-raising" that she and Margaret did over the years. Despite her wild side, she said my mother was also, "very religious, had very long hair that she never cut, and a beautiful singing voice."

Margaret was asked on many occasions to sing and loved Irish songs. When Margaret was in the nursing home and hospital, she clung to a statue of the Blessed Virgin Mary and had holy cards stuffed in her bedclothes.

Mary described Margaret as a very attractive, nice, and fun-loving person. She repeated that Margaret's marriage to Donald O'Connor was not a good one and that he drank a lot. Margaret ended up walking out on him and leaving her large home to move to a small apartment. One Christmas Eve, there was a knock on Margaret's door and she was handed divorce papers.

When we brought up the subject of Geraldine, Mary did not hesitate to tell us what she actually thought of her, and it was not flattering at all. She said, "Geraldine and her daughters took everything Margaret owned." Margaret liked to travel, and while she was still in good health, she would go to New York City each year for the St. Patrick's Day Parade. Funny, I love going to the St. Patrick's Day Parade. Margaret also liked to travel back to Toronto, her birthplace, where she still had family. Margaret always kept her Canadian citizenship and never became an American citizen, although she lived in the United States from age four until her death. Every year she would go to the post office to renew her visa. She never had a driver's license, which explains why she always lived in the same area in Albany. She walked to work, to church, and to the VFW, which she frequented.

Mary told us a story that one evening, herself, Margaret, and Aunt Bea went out to dinner shortly after the family had returned from Italy. Margaret didn't seem like herself and left to go to the ladies' room. That's when Aunt Bea told Mary that Margaret was very upset with her because during their vacation, Aunt Bea had confessed to Margaret that she was her biological mother. According to Mary, Aunt Bea told Margaret that her birth father was someone she loved very much, but because he was not Catholic, her family, being devout Irish Catholics, would never allow such a union.

Beatrice became pregnant, and her sister Mary and her husband, Robert Taggart, immigrated to New York and raised Margaret as their daughter, eventually having two children of their own, Robert Junior and Geraldine. Margaret had asked Aunt Bea if she had any siblings and she was told there were none. I haven't been able to find any documents that say whether Mary Taggart legally adopted Margaret. This was all very interesting information, for here was Margaret finding out that she herself was given up by her birth mother, just as Margaret had done, and the woman she knew her whole life as Aunt Bea was actually her birth mother. So Beatrice is my grandmother.

Mary became quite close to Aunt Bea, who would travel to Albany often to visit. According to both Geraldine and Mary, Beatrice's last name was Crowe. She had only been married once, to someone named Frank who was a police detective in Toronto. Rick and I asked Mary about any relationships Margaret had had over the years; obviously there were a few. We spoke about the fact that Rick and I are just seventeen months apart in age and that someone must have noticed that Margaret was pregnant for two years. We had figured out that Rick and I have different fathers. Mary had a few guesses who Rick's father might be. One was an old friend who lived in Florida, one was a police detective's brother, and one had been a married father with eleven children. Anyways, that is what Mary said.

Mary told us about a photograph of a young man in uniform that Margaret always carried in her wallet. Margaret had told Mary he was the love of her life. Mary was unable to remember his name other than she thought it was the name Freihofer—just like the bakery that originated in Albany. It was definitely a mystery and one that will never be solved. Who was he? Someone I should know about? Her husband? Sadly for Margaret, he was killed in a car accident one Christmas Eve on his way to visit her. At least that is how the story went.

On Mary's lap the whole time we were talking was a clear plastic bag. I kept glancing at it for I could see that it contained photographs. Mary must have noticed me looking at the bag and finally asked, "Would you like to see your mother?"

I couldn't speak. I could barely breathe. I just nodded yes.

She slowly opened the bag and carefully removed

four photographs. Suddenly the air seemed to be sucked out of my lungs. The room was quiet. The only sound I heard was that of my labored breathing and the pounding of my heart. With a shaking hand I reached for the photograph. It was hard to see the image through the tears. When my eyes focused, I realized that I recognized the woman in the photograph. I'd never met her, I'd never seen her before, but I knew her. For the very first time in my life, I could see that I looked like someone. I had such a strong physical and emotional connection to the person I was looking at.

Without saying a word, I handed the picture to Rick. Both of us, with tears in our eyes, just stared at the face of the woman who had given birth to us.

After two-and-a-half hours it was time to say goodbye to Mary. Words could not express what that day meant to me. Thanking Mary and trying to find the words to explain how important this was just didn't seem adequate.

The three of us stood up and walked to the door. Mary hugged me and whispered, "I'm glad that you are Margaret's daughter."

Rick and I walked out the door in stunned silence and got into the car. We just sat there at first, then simultaneously said, "Holy shit!" Our brains were on overload. Mary had given us the photographs to keep so we headed to the nearest drug store to make two copies of each so I could return the originals to Mary. The next stop after that was to the nearest bar.

We ordered a drink and probably would have had more if we both weren't driving. We sat at the bar just trying to process everything we had learned about our birth mother and our brothers. There was definitely a lot to think about. After over an hour, it was time for us to go our separate ways.

Rick headed north and I headed west on the New York State Thruway for the three-hour ride home. The entire time I was replaying the conversation with Mary in my head and reviewing what I had discovered about my biological family. Of all that I had discovered that day, it was trying to get my brain around the fact that at the same time I had been searching for my birth mother, so too were my brothers. They wouldn't have been searching for Rick or me, because they were told, by our mother that there were no other siblings. I found this to be very sad. Had they known about us, had they known of our existence, how very different things might have been.

Arriving home, I called Paul who was in Manhattan working and filled him in on the day's events. I emailed the pictures to him and also to our sons. I took my high school senior picture and placed it next to a picture of Margaret, the first one that Mary had handed to me. I did that because you could see it, the strong resemblance.

Armed with the new information, I was ready to begin a new search for my oldest brothers. I now had two geographic locations New Jersey and Long Island. So how difficult could it be?

MARGARET'S ALBANY HOUSE - 1950s

MARGARET O'CONNOR'S GRAVE

THE FIRST PHOTO I SAW OF MY

BIOLOGICAL MOTHER

ARMED AND FULL OF HOPE

The next morning, after another restless night's sleep, I wrote a thank you letter to Mary expressing our deep gratitude for meeting with us and enclosed the original photographs of Margaret.

I was feeling hopeful with the possibility of finding my brothers. I spent the day looking up telephone numbers on the computer again, returning to the White Pages for anyone with my brothers' names located in New Jersey or Long Island. I wrote each number down and started calling. When I made these calls, I would always start the conversation by saying that I was sorry to bother the person, but I was doing a family search and looking for either a Charles Costantino with a brother named John or I was looking for a John Costantino with a brother named Charles. People were very nice and usually would just say, "You have the wrong number." At least no one ever just hung up on me. I had felt so confident starting the day with my search process narrowed down to just the two states. But I had no luck—not one hit with any of the calls I made.

It was now Thursday morning, September 25. After striking out the previous day, I was starting to feel defeated. I decided to call Mary to recheck the information she had given me regarding my brothers. I just wanted to see if she remembered anything else or if there was something I had missed. Mary seemed genuinely happy to hear from me, but there was nothing she could add to what she had already told us. I still had a few phone numbers remaining. I poured myself another cup of coffee and started calling again.

Over those two days, I must have placed over thirty calls, crossing each name out as I went down the list, making notations next to each one: no one answered, number no longer in service, wrong number. The hours passed quickly, and when I looked up at the clock I noticed that it was now around nine o'clock in the evening. I was feeling as frustrated as hell but decided to dial the last number I had on my list. It was a phone number in New Jersey.

The phone rang and a young woman answered.

With the phone in one hand, my elbow on the kitchen table, and my head resting on my arm, I made the usual introduction as if by rote and stated the reason for my call. "Hi, my name is Susan Moyer, I am sorry to bother you, but I am searching for a Charles Costantino, who has a brother, John."

"Why are you trying to find them?" she asked.

I said that I believed they were my brothers. The woman hesitated a moment, and I was afraid she would be my first hang up, but she just said what everyone else had said to me: "I'm sorry, but I can't help you."

I felt like crying. I was feeling completely mentally and emotionally exhausted, I hung up the phone, slumped back in my chair, and sat there staring into space thinking to myself, *That's it, I can't do this any longer. I'm done, finished.* I still had all of Long Island to call, but I said the hell with it! I gathered up all my paperwork, turned my computer off, and decided to get some much-needed sleep. I made the decision that I would call Rick first thing in the morning and tell him that I was ready to give up.

JACKPOT!

The next morning, Friday, September 26, 2008, I woke up feeling as discouraged as when I went to bed. I looked in the mirror and thought I looked like hell. I washed my face, stumbled downstairs, made a pot of coffee, and sat down at the kitchen table. I then called Rick. As soon as he answered, I told him about all the calls I had made and that I was ready to quit. All of my years of searching were coming to an end. As Rick was listening to me rant, my call waiting beeped with an incoming call. I was annoyed that someone was calling me this early in the morning and interrupting my tirade. Who the heck could this be? I glanced up at the display screen and absolutely could not believe what I was seeing. I had to be dreaming. There was a C. Costantino on the line.

I quickly told Rick what was happening and that I

would call him back. I immediately took the incoming call.

"Hello?"

A young woman's voice asked, "Is this Susan Moyer?"

"Yes," I answered.

She then asked, "Are you looking for a Charles Costantino who has a brother John?"

With my pulse rate quickening, I said, "Yes."

"You called my number and spoke with me last night," she said.

Suddenly I recognized her voice. She was the last person I had spoken with the night before, the very last call that made me decide to call it quits.

What she said next was so unbelievable, so unexpected, that I could barely process what I was hearing. "My name is Carla Costantino," she said. "My father is Charles Costantino, and his brother is John."

I stopped breathing. I needed to sit down. I was

shaking so badly I nearly dropped the phone. I actually said to her, "I need a moment."

Carla said that I had "completely shocked her" and that she had needed to speak with her parents after I called her. Remember, my brothers had no idea that they had siblings, so when I called it just didn't make any sense to her. I then told Carla that actually there were two siblings: myself, and a brother named Richard. I told her a little about how Rick and I had found each other just three years ago and how I had been searching for my biological family for over twenty years. Before Carla called me, she had done a little research on her own to see what she could find out about me. She still had my number on her caller ID from the night before. It was a little creepy when she asked me if I lived in the white house with the jeep in the driveway. You have to love Google Earth!

We were both talking fast and asking a lot of questions. It was verbal chaos. She told me that she just happened to have her father's old telephone number and that he actually lived in a neighboring town. It was just a sheer stroke of luck that I even had called that number—and in fact, I had been spelling their name wrong, for I had been looking up the name Constantino and it is actually Costantino. Carla told me that my brother John did live out on Long Island with his wife, Lucy. This life-changing phone call went on for quite a while. Finally we exchanged emails and hung up.

First I called Rick. I'm surprised he understood a word I was saying in my frenzied state as I blurted everything out. There was shock and euphoria coming through the telephone from the other end. My second telephone call was to Paul who was sitting in a meeting in his office in Manhattan. I needed to tell him everything. He asked me to slow down so he could understand what I was saying. Paul was so happy and excited for me. Next I called my sons to tell them that I had found their uncles.

I had done it! I had really done it! I found them—
and to think that I was ready to call it quits and not search
anymore that very morning. It was that last phone call I
had made the previous night that was the right number.
Unbelievable! I then called all my friends and my cousin
Pat. I ran to my computer and Carla was already sending
me pictures of my brothers and their families. As fast as
she was sending them, I was forwarding them to Paul,
Jeff, and Jason. I was staring at the computer screen in
total disbelief that I was actually looking at the faces of
my brothers for the very first time.

The telephone rang again and this time the screen
read L. Costantino. "Hello?" I said.

The voice on the other end said, "Hello Susan, this is
your sister-in-law, Lucy, your brother John's wife."

For the next several hours there were numerous
phone calls and emails. I learned a little about my brothers growing up in Brooklyn and what a rough childhood

they'd had. It was not long after our mother abandoned them that their father left them. Their elderly Italian paternal grandparents kept and raised them. If it weren't for them, they would have been left on the street or placed in an orphanage. Sadly, their grandmother passed away several years later, but their beloved grandfather kept them together. Lucy confirmed what Mary had told me: that she had hired a private investigator and that is how they had found Margaret in 1998 right before her death.

I told Lucy about my family and how Rick and I had found each other. She told me about her life with John and that he has two daughters from previous marriages. She said that John was retired and his hobby was buying and restoring classic cars. Now that was a really interesting bit of information, because Rick has the same hobby. In fact, as it turned out, they had similar models of classic cars. How's that for a coincidence?

I lost track of how many times I called Paul, who

was still trying to conduct a meeting. He finally had to apologize to everyone in the room for all the interruptions from his wife and explained all the telephone calls. One man sitting with Paul said that he should call Oprah and tell my story. My sons were very excited about all the new developments. Everyone who heard the news was thrilled for me—everyone, that is, but my mother.

She continued to be the one person in my life who was told nothing of my discoveries. I was keeping secrets from her, just as she had done with me and I hated it. I have come to the realization over the years that I am indeed hurt, very disappointed, and yes, somewhat angry with her. The irony is that she never suspected anything. What seemed to be her greatest fear—that our relationship would suffer or change in some way if I were to find my brothers or any member of my biological family—never happened. Nothing changed for her since I met Rick, although a lot has definitely changed for me. I had led a

double life: my life with her and my new life with the discovery of my brothers. She was now nearing ninety years
of age, and to tell her everything now seemed pointless.
How sad, that she should not rejoice and share in my happiness.

Exact Search Results - U.S. Public Records Index
You searched for **Charles Constantino** Refine your search

All Directories & Member Lists Results

View Record	Name	Age	Street address	City	State	ZIP	Phone	Record Number
View Record	Charles Constantino			Clifton	New Jersey	07012		368410372
View Record	Charles F Constantino	66	disc	Pequannock	New Jersey	07440		725375818
View Record	Charles F Constantino	66	wrg	Wayne	New Jersey	07470		714255477
View Record	Charles J Constantino	78		Clifton	New Jersey	07012		42853255
View Record	Charles J Constantino	49		Clifton	New Jersey	07012		704755261
View Record	Charles J Constantino	50	dis	Hopatcong	New Jersey	07843		509957066

Results per page 10

You are here: Historical Records > Directories & Member Lists > U.S. Public Records Index

PHONE LISTING

207

ROLLER COASTERS AND BIRTHDAY WISHES

After so many years of searching, I had accomplished what had once seemed impossible: I had found my brothers. But where would I go from here? I had been in constant contact with Carla and Lucy but had not spoken with either Charles or John. Were they interested in meeting me? Did they even care that they had a sister?

It turned out that at the same time that I was adjusting to everything, they were adjusting to the fact that they had two siblings they had not known existed. They were also dealing with all the revived raw emotions and animosity they felt toward Margaret. I understood that. If they chose not to meet me, that was okay, for at least I had found them. And after fifty-five years of not having them in my life, I could live with that.

One evening, shortly after all the news broke, Paul

and I had dinner at Scalinatella in Manhattan. Paul was telling Marco, one of the owners, about all the recent events in my life. Marco told Paul we could use his restaurant as a meeting place for my family if we wanted. I couldn't think of a better location. But would everyone agree to do this? The city was geographically an ideal location for all of us to meet. But could I actually get my whole family—all three of my brothers—together? I had no idea, but time would tell and I was going to give it my best shot.

I called Rick and told him about our plan. Of course he didn't hesitate. I called both Jeff and Jason. Jason was already living in the city, but Jeff was coaching college football in Upstate New York, and it was the middle of football season. I told Jeff that under no circumstances would this family reunion happen without him and that he was to explain the situation to his boss.

Next I had to find out if Charles and John were interested in meeting—not so easy. The emotional roller-coaster ride was to continue. My brother John was the most reluctant, because he has such anger and bitterness toward our mother. Charles was a little more willing and interested in getting together. All of this was being handled between myself, Carla and Lucy. I still hadn't spoken to John or Charles. My birthday was in a few weeks. It would mark the third anniversary of Rick and I meeting. What an amazing birthday it would be once again if this time all three of my brothers and I were together.

We chose the date of Sunday, October 26, 2008, with Scalinatella as the location. Everyone was on board except John. Lucy and I had been on the phone numerous times and she told me to just be patient. John would come around.

Finally it was Friday, the eleventh of October, the day before my birthday. I said to Rick that if John was not interested in meeting us, "then so be it." It was not worth all the coaxing if he truly did not want to come. It had to come from his heart.

Around five o'clock on Friday evening, the phone rang, and once again it was Lucy. The first thing she said was, "Happy birthday, Susan, your brothers will be there on the twenty-sixth."

Tears sprang into my eyes and I asked Lucy what had changed John's mind. It seems that Charles had called him and told him that he was definitely going, and that John should put aside his anger at our mother and come meet his brother and sister. Charles told him that Rick and I had nothing to do with what Margaret had done to them.

So the date, the time, and the location were now confirmed. In a couple of weeks, after all these years, I was going to meet my two oldest brothers. It was really going to happen. The four of us would come together for the very first time.

A FAMILY UNITED

Someone says, "They're here," and all eyes focus back on the stairwell. Descending the stairs is someone I have only been able to fantasize and dream of meeting—my brother John. The first thing we all notice is the similarity between John and Rick. Although John is taller, there is a strong resemblance in their hair color, the shape of their faces, and their eyes. Lucy, who was so instrumental in helping to make this meeting possible, is standing beside him. She is petite, with dark hair and a lovely face. John looks as nervous as I am. I step forward slowly and approach him with much trepidation, for I am not sure how to greet him.

I ask if I can hug him, and he says "Yes," so I do. I whisper to John, "I am not Margaret," and when he looks at me, he knows what I am trying to tell him.

I step aside and Rick comes forward and gives his big brother a hug. I introduce John and Lucy to Paul, Jeffrey, and Jason. Rick introduces Colette, Andrea, and her fiancé, Tony. We then all congregate around the bar for those much-needed cocktails and await the arrival of my other special guest.

Within minutes, all eyes revert back to the stairwell, and there is the final piece of the puzzle—my brother Charles, along with his daughter, Carla. Charles is shorter than John, has gray hair, and is thin. A number of years ago, he had his larynx removed, so he has difficulty speaking. Charles is the oldest of the four of us, the one with the memories of our mother—the one who clearly remembers her saying goodbye, saying, "I'll be back for you."

Carla is an energetic, vibrant person. She has long blond hair and an outgoing personality. She makes us all feel that we belong here, that this is right, that this was meant to be. Again, there are more hugs and introductions. The most emotional for me was introducing my brothers to their two nephews, my sons. The feeling of awkwardness is obvious amongst the four of us. We are family coming together under very unusual circumstances, so where would we begin? Where does one start with a lifetime of information and questions?

We start with the one common denominator in our lives, our birth mother, Margaret.

Lucy has sweetly put photo albums together and given Rick and me each one with pictures of our mother at various ages. There are pictures of John and Charles when they were young. We all intently study each photograph to find physical similarities. There is one in particular we examine: a black and white snapshot of Margaret in her late teens or early twenties on Coney Island. In what I assume to be her handwriting it says, "To Charlie, Love Margie." When Jeff sees it, I hear him say to Carla, "That looks like my mother."

All I can think is, Wow.

At one point it seems like everyone is talking at once, different conversations going on throughout the restaurant. I sit myself down next to Charles. He is self-conscious about speaking, but I reassure him that I can understand him just fine. Cameras are flashing and someone is video recording the whole event.

It is now, time for dinner, which is served family style. Paul and I had chosen our favorite dishes ahead of time. Sitting to my left is my niece, Andrea; Paul is to my right, and across from me there is Jeff with his new cousin Carla by his side, with Charles sitting on her right.

Before we start to eat, Paul stands to makes a speech. "What a very special day this is. Susan has been waiting a very long time for this moment. Thank you, everyone, for coming, and here's to many more meals together in the future."

We bow our heads in grace, and then our large Italian—slightly Irish—feast begins.

SIBLINGS UNITED AT SCALINATELLA

WITH MY BROTHER CHARLES

DNA AND THE UNEXPECTED

Sometimes when you are not expecting it, the unexpected can happen. A lot of time had passed since that family dinner in Manhattan, and there have also been many changes in my life. Paul's work took us from having the apartment in New York City to having a place in Saratoga Springs, New York. By 2014, I pretty much thought that I had come to the end of my journey. There wasn't anything new that I could possibly do or find pertaining to my biological family. Finding my birth father or any family member on his side would simply be impossible.

Then one day in June when I was on the computer, I noticed an advertisement on Ancestry for DNA tests.

Over the years I had thought about taking a DNA test. My brother Rick and I had even discussed it, but never got around to ordering one. I still had an immense curiosity in my genetic background and if I possibly had any more biological family connections.

I requested a test. The kit arrived within a week and all I had to do was give a saliva sample and mail it back. I did. Simple enough.

I had completely forgotten about the DNA test until the morning of August 14 when I went on the Ancestry website. A message appeared telling me that my DNA results were in. I was excited to see the results. If my goal was to find more biological family members, I was successful. A list of dozens of matches appeared. The first person on the list said that we were close to first cousins, and every other match was a third or fourth cousin. This person was a female but there were no names, just a code.

This close relative had a family tree so I took a look at it. There wasn't one name on it that I recognized, but that is nothing new. Over my years of searching, I also always checked geographic locations because I did not have a name to go by. I looked to see if there were any connections to the Albany area. Surprisingly, on this person's tree Albany was listed. Okay, so that was something. I decided to write a brief message explaining that we connected closely on Ancestry. I wrote a little about myself, and my connection to Albany and hit the send button.

Later that day, a message appeared from the person I had written to. It said that it was very likely that we were related on our father's side. She was also adopted.

Are you kidding me? What is it about my family having children then putting them up for adoption?

Her name was Natalie*. She had found her biological mother's family a few years ago after searching for a long time. I learned that she was born in Albany and put up for adoption. The note said that she lived outside Saratoga Springs. Now this was getting stranger by the moment. She referenced another person that showed up as a third cousin to both of us and she had been in touch but this person—ready for this—was also adopted. What the heck!

We shared telephone numbers and planned to talk later in the evening. Around seven o'clock, I called. She shared with me personal information about herself and her family. She was also born at Brady Maternity Hospital, just as I had been. She is five years younger than me. And she too was put into St. Catherine's Center for Children for adoption. Pretty amazing. We were thinking we could be first cousins, but weren't sure exactly how we were connected.

Because she had a lot of information on her birth mother, she knew that we were related through our birth father. Like me, Natalie had discovered that her birth mother was deceased, and she had discovered her biological siblings. Then she told me that her birth mother's name was Margaret, though definitely not the same Margaret who gave birth to me. What a coincidence that both of our mothers' names are Margaret!

If anyone is familiar with the old television show *The Twilight Zone*, I felt like I had just entered it. I told Natalie about my journey and about my brother Rick, who lived just north of where she lives. I explained how Rick and I came together and that he was also born at Brady Maternity Hospital. After I was done with my story, she paused then asked me if there had been an article in a local paper about Rick and me several years ago.

"Yes," I said.

"I have the article. I saved it," Natalie said. "And I spoke to your brother."

"What?" I asked.

This article was published on my brother shortly after we had met our brothers in New York. Natalie saw and saved it. It was about adoptees, and it struck a chord with her. Natalie went on to say how she looked up my brother from the article and actually called him. She wanted to ask him how he found his siblings, because at the time she had not yet found her biological family. By now you know coincidence has played a big part in my story, but this was stranger than any coincidence—my newfound relative on my birth father's side had spoken to my brother Rick on my birth mother's side.

Later that night, I called Rick. I told him about my conversation with Natalie and that she had seen the article and that he had talked to her. He was dumbfounded. He did not remember the conversation with her, but he had received numerous phone calls regarding the article

Talking to Natalie, I told her that I came across a man in my research and I wondered if he could be my father. According to the records, he lived north of Albany and was a high school graduate and a truck driver. I told her the name and it turns out that she too had thought he could be her father. She'd even contacted the man's family and asked this person's daughter to take a DNA test—which she agreed to—but it showed that there was no biological connection.

We shared more information about each other. Like myself, Natalie has two sons. She's an artist and a teacher. I found out that when Natalie was in college, she had a boyfriend from Rochester and would visit here frequently—and not only that: her son even had gone to the University of Rochester for a semester.

She asked if I had done DNA testing on any other site. I hadn't. She told me that she was on GEDMatch and Family Tree DNA, where I could upload my DNA results. Natalie put me in touch with a friend of this third cousin, we both connected with, who could help me figure out how to upload my results. I received an email from the friend named Sandy, who explained how to upload the information.

I sat down one night and tried to figure it out but didn't have much luck. Finally, the next day I was notified that my uploads were successful and that I should receive the results in three to five days.

I was heading to Saratoga on Tuesday, August 19 so Natalie and I could meet for the first time. My grandson was due to be born around that time so I told her I would be there unless the baby arrived. Paul and I were at the lake having dinner when on Saturday night when Jeff called to say that Anna's water had broken. We were off to Pittsburgh.

On the way there, I contacted Natalie to tell her that our first meeting was going to be delayed. My grandson was on his way.

The following Friday, I drove back up to the lake for the weekend. Paul was arriving from Saratoga around five. I was sitting out on the deck when Paul got there. He was carrying his bag inside when he told me my phone was going off. I ran into the kitchen to get it and there was a text message from Natalie. The Family Finder DNA results were in. We were not first cousins. We we're SISTERS.

I quickly took Paul's computer and opened up my email. Sure enough, the DNA showed that Natalie and I were half-sisters, not first cousins. My phone rang and it was Natalie. The two of us were crying and in shock. Sisters—now that was a new word for me to get my mind around. I had never in a million years thought I would ever have a connection to my birth father, or a sister. Even when I decided to take the DNA test, it never occurred to me that there would be biological discoveries that would lead me in that direction.

Natalie and I met for the first time on Tuesday, August 26, 2014, in Saratoga. I arrived first and told the hostess I was meeting my sister for the first time and requested a table off to the side where we could have some privacy. "Plan on us being here for quite awhile," I said.

Shortly after I was seated, Natalie walked in. I don't know if it was because this was my third time doing this, or if it was because she was a sister, but I was calm and relaxed. Our three-hour lunch was wonderful. It is so hard trying to fit a lifetime of conversation into a brief meeting.

Natalie had been back to St. Catherine's just as I had, but now we planned to go together. This would be my third time there. The first was in 1998 when I drove myself there and began my very long journey of discovery. The second time was with my brother Rick. A lot had happened in my life since that first visit.

The next day, Natalie and I met in Albany then drove together back to where our lives began. We did not have an appointment but managed to briefly meet with the director. Of course, as we pleaded our cases, all she said— just like everyone has been saying for years— "Sorry, but I can't tell you anything."

Several weeks later, when I was back in Saratoga, Paul and I went to have lunch at my sister's house. After that, I decided that I wanted to have my sister and brother meet each other, so I set up a dinner at our apartment for later in the month.

On a Saturday evening, Natalie and her husband and Rick and Colette all arrived at our place. It was interesting and emotional to be standing in our kitchen with my brother and sister. Paul looked at the three of us and said, "Okay, so this is your brother and this is your sister from a different mother. You are related to both of them but they are not related to each other."

What can I say? No matter how we all came to be, or how we all arrived at this point in our lives ... we are family.

NORTH OF THE BORDER: CANADIAN CONNECTIONS

Through the four DNA websites that I continue to use, I have learned that I am related to a lot of people—and I mean a lot. This just amazes me. I connected with a cousin named Mike, who lives in Canada. He is related to me through my birth mother, and was very open to sharing family information. Another person in particular that I have connected with is my cousin Kathleen who lives in the Toronto area, the city where my birth mother was born. Kathleen knew my grandmother Beatrice very well; Beatrice was her father's first cousin and was her sponsor for Confirmation. But Kathleen never knew that Beatrice had a daughter named Margaret. She was shocked to learn the story of my mother.

My great-grandmother Mary Agnes Hynes and Kathleen's father were brother and sister. I sent Kathleen a few pictures I had, including ones of Beatrice, and she confirmed that is who it was. Kathleen shared a wealth of information with me, including many photographs of other family members and stories.

One item I had not been able to find anywhere was my grandmother's obituary. I was very curious to see when she died and what names were mentioned as her survivors. One evening, an email appeared from Kathleen telling me that she found Beatrice's obituary while going through her mother's things. She attached an image of it to the email. She'd died in 1987. It said she was the "loving aunt" to Mrs. Margaret O'Connor and Mrs. Geraldine Mayer, both of Albany, New York.

Loving aunt—the same words used to describe my mother Margaret in her obituary in 1998. Most interesting was the fact that Beatrice did not acknowledge Margaret as her daughter, just as Margaret did not acknowledge me as hers. We will never know the story behind the circumstances of why Beatrice let her sister Mary move to New York City and raise Margaret as her daughter. Just add that to the long list of unanswerable questions.

On May 21, 2016, Paul and I drove to Toronto to meet Kathleen and her husband for the first time. After months of communicating by email and text, I was looking forward to the trip. Kathleen had a whole itinerary planned for the weekend. We met at a hotel, and Paul and I got in the back seat to begin our day of discovery, including meeting new family members. Kathleen had an envelope brimming with pictures of my relatives, including grandparents, aunts, uncles, and cousins. It was simply amazing to be looking at the faces of all these relatives. Kathleen handed Paul another picture and asked him who, he thought I looked like out of the group of women. Paul pointed to one and Kathleen agreed and said, "That was Aunt Mary."

Kathleen handed me a clear eight by twelve plastic

envelope. Curious, I pulled out the twenty-five typed written pages on thin opaque paper. At the top of the first page was the title "Victims of the Stoolpigeon." Kathleen said it was Frank Crowe's (Beatrice's husband's) original manuscript for a book he was writing in 1973. There were also three letters from a woman who was editing the book. Knowing that I was writing a book, Kathleen said that she wanted me to have it. What a meaningful gift, and how special it made me feel that she would entrust me with it after having kept it for so long.

Our first stop was to meet several cousins for lunch. It was nice to meet my cousin Mike, with whom I had been in contact, and his family including his father. From there we went to the family cemetery, where we visited my great-grandmother's grave and the grave of my grandmother Beatrice. Standing over Beatrice's grave was pretty amazing, just as it had been when I stood over my mother's. We all got back in the car and our sightseeing tour of the area continued with a stop at Beatrice's house. I learned that she loved horse racing and the water. Her home was in the beaches area on the shore of Lake Ontario. This is significant in many ways, for I have spent my entire life on Lake Ontario loving the water, and Paul and I are part owners of a racehorse in Saratoga.

After several hours of riding around in the back of the car, I noticed that Paul's eyes were starting to glaze over. It had been a long day and had been a lot to take in, mentally and emotionally. My head was spinning. It was late afternoon and I asked if we could stop somewhere for a cocktail. Etzio, Kathleen's husband, was more than happy to oblige. We found a place to park in front of a pub near Beatrice's house and ordered four Guinnesses.

After that, we drove back to the other side of Toronto and they dropped us off at the hotel to freshen up before meeting again for dinner a little later in the evening. Kathleen brought a package of more photographs and a copy of a family tree that was put together by her mother and none other than Beatrice in 1984. Kathleen also included all the postcards and letters that she had received from Beatrice over the years. After dinner, Paul and I went back to the hotel and I emptied out the contents of the envelope on a coffee table. I sat there for a couple of hours just reading and looking at everything. Reading all the letters and postcards from Beatrice gave me an insight into the woman. They were warm and lovingly written.

Sunday morning arrived and we headed over to Kathleen's house for brunch. Kathleen had invited two more of my cousins, as well as their husbands, to join us. It was a beautiful warm sunny day as we sat outside on the patio. Although I had missed out on being a part of this family, I felt very comfortable and welcomed. They all grew up together and have a history together. They all knew Beatrice and described her as such a warm, loving person.

Everyone was interested in my story and what I knew of Beatrice and Margaret, which of course was not much. It was still shocking for them to learn that Beatrice had a daughter.

It was time for Paul and I to leave and head home back over the border. Right before heading out, Kathleen said one of the nicest and most touching things: "I think Aunt Bea would be thrilled that you are here."

I cannot thank Kathleen enough for everything she has shared and planned over the past several months and what it has meant to me. A number of years ago, I had gone to Toronto with Paul and searched through the Canadian archives in search of my birth family. I came home empty-handed. But this time I returned home with both a family history and a feeling of belonging.

FAMILY BRUNCH WITH COUSINS IN TORONTO

WITH MY FEMALE COUSINS IN TORONTO

THE END OF MY JOURNEY . . .
OR SO I THOUGHT

I had come to the end of my journey—or at least it seemed that way. I hadn't been doing any further searching. As far as I was concerned, I had all the information regarding my birth family that I was ever going to have.

But then I received a telephone call from my sister on the morning of Friday, February 24, 2017. Natalie had just had a conversation with Sandy saying she was pretty confident that she had figured out who our birth father was: "We have a name," she excitedly exclaimed.

His name was Kenneth L. Palmer.

Sadly, Kenneth had tragically passed away at age forty-four in 1974 in Albany, New York. Over the next few days, there were numerous emails and telephone calls. Sandy had uncovered the names of my father's siblings, parents, twelve first cousins, and five generations of ancestors. I learned that two of Kenneth's siblings were still alive. We also discovered that Kenneth had been in the Coast Guard during WWII and married twice, which produced four (on the record) children. The amount of information and paperwork Sandy sent was staggering.

There are no words of gratitude to thank Sandy for everything she has done. What she accomplished is nothing short of miraculous.

With a little investigating online, I came up with a telephone number for Kenneth's sister named Marie who was ninety-four years old. It had been a long time since I had made random phone calls but I thought I'd give it a go. So on Wednesday evening, March 1, I dialed the number and a woman answered.

I asked if I had the right person and she said, "Yes."

I asked if she had had a brother named Kenneth.

"Yes," she said.

I then told her that I had just learned that Kenneth

was my father and I told her my story.

"Oh, you are Kenny's daughter?"

"Yes," I answered.

She was warm and friendly. I shared with her what information I had. She told me the story of her mother, my grandmother, who had immigrated from Ireland to New York City. She told me how my grandmother, Elizabeth met her husband, my grandfather, Oliver. She shared that Elizabeth was from Wicklow, Ireland. Marie talked about how heartbroken Elizabeth was when Kenny left home and moved to Albany. I asked her if she knew of any of his other children, and she said she knew of one. I did not want to press her too much for information, for after all, she is ninety-four years old.

I was told my father was buried in a cemetery in Coxsackie, New York, where the family was from. I gave her my telephone number and asked if it would be okay if I called her again and she said yes. I immediately called

Natalie and told her of my conversation with our aunt. She had just gotten off the phone with a cousin of ours who had also shared some information about our father. This cousin verified that our father had been married two times and had four children: Two daughters with his first wife and two children with his second wife. Okay, so now I was up to four new siblings.

On Ancestry, Sandy had found Kenneth's marriage record to a person named Janet, his second wife. They did have two children together, a son and a daughter. Now it was confirmed that I had a second sister and another brother. Unbelievable! With some more digging, I found her maiden name and learned that she had remarried. Sandy found Janet on Facebook. I looked her up and just stared at the photographs of the woman who had been married to my father. WOW!

I did another White Pages search and came up with a telephone number for Janet. So on Thursday, March 2, I took a deep breath and dialed the phone number. A woman answered and I asked if it was Janet. "No, I am her daughter."

I told her who I was and asked if her mother had been married to a Kenneth Palmer.

"Yes."

I told her that I had just discovered that Kenneth was my birth father.

She said, "That would make my sister, Kimberly, and my brother, Kenneth, your siblings." Why, yes, it would! Trying to process this information was astounding.

She said her mother was down South until April but she would give her sister my information and telephone number. I told her that I was on Facebook and her sister could check me out there. She said it was completely up to her sister and her mother if they wanted to reach out to me. I understood that. I thanked her and hung up. I suddenly realized that I was so nervous that I had given her the wrong cell number. Stupid! I was so embarrassed, but I had to call her back with the correct number. She laughed.

A little while later, I was standing in the kitchen preparing dinner when my cell phone rang. It was a 518 area code, the Albany area. I answered and a woman asked if I was Susan. "Yes," I said.

"This is Kimberly." She said she messaged me on Facebook as soon as her sister called but couldn't wait for me to reply so she picked up the phone. As with similar conversations, it started out with trying to tell my whole story and how I got to her as briefly as possible, which frankly is impossible. Kimberly was very warm and friendly and told me about our birth father and about her life.

Paul walked in while I was on the phone. I grabbed a piece of paper and wrote that I was speaking with my sister Kimberly. He smiled and left the room. I am sure he was thinking, "Great, Susan has more siblings." Paul has continued to be right by my side throughout all these years and throughout all these discoveries.

I asked Kimberly if she would be interested in meeting and I was thrilled when she said yes. We set a date for a week later on March 11 when I would be in Saratoga. I called Natalie and shared my conversation with our sister and told her the date for all of us to meet. Later in the evening, Kimberly and I were texting back and forth. Paul and I were driving to Pittsburgh the next morning to see Jeff, Anna, and our grandson Ethan.

On our drive home Sunday, my phone went off. It was a text message from Kimberly, along with a photograph. It was of my birth father, Kenneth. For the first time in my life, I was looking at my father's face. It took sixty-three years, but there he was. I made some sort of audible sound and Paul asked what was wrong. "It's a picture of my father," I said. I immediately forwarded the photo to Natalie then texted Kimberly to thank her.

On Monday, I was texting with my sisters to pick a location where we could all meet. Paul had set up a private room at a hotel near his office in Clifton Park, which was a convenient location for all of us. It was nice to have a somewhat private setting for something like this instead of a restaurant. In one of Kimberly's texts, she wrote that her mother believed that she knew my birth mother, Margaret. Now that threw me. Her mother knew Margaret? On Tuesday night, I called Kimberly to confirm a time for Saturday but I said I could not wait until Saturday to know the story of how her mother knew my mother.

She asked me if my mother had been married to a Donald O'Connor.

"Yes," I said.

She then went on to say that her mother's second husband, Kimberly's stepfather and father to Kimberly's younger sisters, was close friends with Donald O'Connor and that when Kimberly was young, her parents and her brother use to go to my mother's house. In fact, Margaret was godmother to her younger sister. For a few seconds I didn't say anything. I couldn't. I needed to process what I was just told.

Kimberly then said that the other day her mother had told her an interesting bit of information. One night, after a few cocktails at Margaret's house, Margaret confided to Kimberly's mother that she had had a little girl with Kenneth and given her up for adoption.

That would be me. I was finally acknowledged. That powerful bit of information, confirmed beyond any doubt, who my birth parents were.

So, Kenneth is definitely my father and Kimberly and her brother, Kenneth, are my siblings. Just as I had years ago when Carla called to tell me that Charles was her father and John was her uncle, I said to Kimberly that I needed a moment to process what she just told me.

Heck, I needed more than a moment. We hung up and I immediately called Natalie. My next phone call was to my brother Rick to share with him what Kim had just told me. Rick answered the phone. "Are you sitting down?" I asked.

"As a matter of fact I am." He said.

"Good, because you are not going to believe this," I said.

March 11, 2017, arrived, the date when Natalie and I would meet our sister Kimberly. When you are meeting a family member for the first time, it is so personal, so surreal, and emotions run extremely high. Paul and I arrived first, followed by Natalie and her husband. Natalie and I were deep in conversation when Paul looked out the glass door entry to the room and said, "I think that's your sister."

I looked up, and yes, there stood Kimberly. She was shaking with nerves and tears streaming down her face. I threw my arms around her, telling her it was okay. When I released my grip on her, I stepped back and was astonished to see that we have the exact same color green eyes. There was an instant connection. Natalie came forward to hugged Kim and then Paul and Natalie's husband followed suit. We all sat down at the long wooden table to begin our conversation.

Two hours had passed since we sat down. Kimberly had to head back to Albany. I asked Kim if she wanted to meet again, and I was thrilled when she said yes. The plan now was for Paul and I and Natalie and her husband to drive in separate cars down to Coxsackie, which was about forty-five minutes away. We were going to meet our father.

Kenneth was buried in Riverside Cemetery located on the Hudson River. Paul and I arrived first, and according to the vague directions Marie had given me, I knew we had to turn left into the cemetery then turn right.

What I didn't know was where exactly the grave was located. Natalie arrived, and the four of us spread out reading each headstone we came upon looking for Kenneth. The wind was really blowing and the temperatures were a balmy thirty-two degrees, with the wind chill seemingly minus something. God, it was cold.

I had been told that Kenneth was buried next to his mother, my grandmother Elizabeth, so after checking out a good number of headstones, I headed in one direction by myself, and with a lot of luck—or maybe I was being guided—I found Kenneth.

I yelled to Paul, who was on top of a knoll. He then shouted over to Natalie that I'd found Kenneth. They came running over and there we stood, staring down at the grave of the person who had evaded us for so long— our father. Natalie started to cry, saying she couldn't believe that we'd found him. I put my arms around her and there we stood huddled together, shaking from the bitter cold and probably nerves. We had found him, along with our grandmother. We would have stayed longer, but the bitter cold got the better of us, so we headed back to our cars and said our goodbyes.

On our way back to Saratoga, I sent Kim pictures of the headstones. She had never been to Kenneth's grave. She told me later that when she shared with her mother that we had gone to the cemetery, her mother said she was surprised, for Kenneth had told her he wanted to be cremated and have his ashes scattered over the water. That gave me chills, for those are my same wishes.

I was happy knowing that I would see Kimberly again in a few weeks. Paul and I had a few trips planned. First we were leaving for the Bahamas on March 26 for a week, then we'd be home for a week before a trip to Tampa on Sunday, April 9. On Saturday, I was running around trying to get things done to get ready to catch a flight early the next morning. I had left my phone charging on the kitchen counter when I stopped and looked at it and saw that I had several new emails.

I noticed one email was from someone named Julie and it was written to both Natalie and myself, so that piqued my interest. I took a moment to read it. She said she was writing on behalf of her mother, Sharon—someone I didn't know. From reading further, I figured out her mother's initials were S.B. This was a person who showed up on Ancestry DNA back in October as a match to Natalie and me. She was a half-sister. Back then, both Natalie and I had written to S.B. through Ancestry but never heard back. We just left it that it was someone who did not want to communicate; either they were adopted or they had a relationship with our father and were not thrilled to know that he had other children. Julie went on to say that her mother had not been on Ancestry in a long time, but she had read the emails that Natalie and I had sent months ago. Her mother was adopted and knew nothing about her biological parents. Interestingly, Sharon was born and adopted in Massachusetts. Now that surely is a mystery. Another sibling who was adopted.

Julie said her mother was now ready to get in touch with us—or at least she told Julie that she could reach out. Then I read that Julie and her parents live in Rochester.

What? They live in the same city that I live in?

Everyone else lived in the Albany area or down near New York City. This was incredible.

After reading the email, I texted Natalie and told her to check her email. She called me a little while later and we both were in shock that S.B. had reached out. Frankly we had given up on that ever happening. Later in the day I wrote back to Julie, telling her about myself, and the recent discovery of my birth father. She wrote back asking a few more questions. I was happy to share everything that I knew.

Julie and I continued to email back and forth, and in one of them she said that her mother was willing to meet me. We chose the date of May 17th. I was glad that Sharon wanted to meet. In the meantime I called my dear friend Robby to see if she would like to take a girls' road trip to Saratoga and meet my sisters. She did not hesitate. So on Thursday, April 26, Robby and I headed east. The trip went fast as the two of us did a lot of talking and laughing the whole way. The plan was to have my sisters Natalie and Kimberly meet at the apartment around five then walk across the street to have dinner.

Kim arrived first, followed shortly after by Natalie. It was so much fun to be sitting around the kitchen counter laughing and sharing stories with my sisters. Robby said she just sat back to take it all in. She knew me when I did not even think I had any siblings.

I mentioned to Kimberly that the DNA test results from a test she took should be in sometime in the next two weeks. I had an extra DNA test and had mailed it to her when she agreed to take one. She looked at me and said, "You know, I really didn't want to take the test." "I didn't want to learn that you weren't my sister." I thought that was the sweetest thing for her to say. It really touched me.

The evening was spectacular, and I asked Kim if she would join Natalie and me in June when Sandy and Eileen were going to be in Saratoga. She said she would.

On the evening of May 9, I was working on the computer when I received a text from Natalie asking if Kim's DNA results had come in. I told her no, but we expected them at any time. Within an hour, I received notification from Ancestry that Kim's DNA results were in. I stopped what I was doing and logged into Ancestry. Although feeling 99.9 percent confident that Kim was my sister, there was just that little bit of doubt. I clicked on the results— for like Kim, I did not want to learn that she wasn't my sister.

And then, there it was. The DNA proved that she was my sister. I couldn't have been happier. From the moment we met, I'd felt a strong bond. It also showed that Kim was a half-sister not only to Natalie and I, but also to Sharon. I immediately called Natalie to tell her the DNA results and said I was going to call Kim, but it went to Kim's voice mail. In the meantime, Natalie, in all of her excitement, had texted Kim. Kim called me within fifteen minutes and I told her the wonderful news. I think we both took a deep happy sigh of relief.

Between traveling and all the events in my life, I realized that I had not filled Jason in on all the latest developments. I called him with the updates and mentioned Sharon and her daughter Julie and they lived in Rochester. I then sent him pictures including one of Julie that I had found on Facebook. He was sitting with his girlfriend Maura and was sharing everything with her. Then Jason replied that Maura knows Julie. She went to high school with her. Throughout my journey there have been so many serendipitous moments. This certainly was another one added to the list.

Paul and I had gone to Pittsburgh to visit Jeff and his family and while there I received a text message from Jason saying that he had met his cousin Julie the night before. Jason and Maura were out with a group of friends bowling when Julie had spotted Maura. She came over and that is when Maura introduced Julie to her newfound cousin Jason. It is still so strange to me that I have biological family living in Rochester.

May 17th arrived, the day I would meet Sharon and her daughter Julie. I set up a reservation at a local restaurant. Paul and Maura were out of town on business so Jason said he would go with me. Jason and I arrived at the restaurant first. We were standing by the front door speaking when Julie walked in with her mother, Sharon, my newest sibling.

We warmly greeted each other, then the four of us sat down. It seems funny that this was my fifth first-time meeting with a new sibling. You may think it would get old and that I would not have the same emotions with each introduction, but on many levels I do. My initial thought is that I am still amazed that I have come this far—that this "lonely child" is sitting with a new-found sibling. I am still amazed that my journey of search has brought me to this place in my life, when I had thought for so many years that I would never have the opportunity to meet even one sibling.

Both, Sharon and Julie were very inquisitive about my story. Sharon asked questions about our birth father and family, including our other siblings. I answered everything she asked. But knowing from Julie that her mother is quite cautious and a little skeptical, I treaded lightly and did not push her on anything. It is totally up to each individual, how they want to process and proceed with the discovery of new family members. I am respectful of that, for as I have mentioned before, I never wanted to intrude on someone's life.

Julie and I remain in contact and have seen each other a several times. Jason and Maura have also run into Julie. Sharon and I have only been in contact with each other once since we met, and that is okay. I had let her know that if she ever feels differently and would like to reach out, I will be there.

MEETING/HUGGING KIM FOR FIRST TIME

EPILOGUE

So this is my story, the story of my long journey searching for my biological family. Along the way, there were many surprises, tears, fears, frustration, and discouragement, but most of all determination. In the end, there was much joy and jubilation. A lot of hard work, time, and sheer willpower went into the final result, and yes, it was all worth it. Each time I would discover any new bit of information, I considered it a gift. I never had any expectations of what I would find. I did not want to set myself up for disappointment or hurt in either what I found or in what I did not find.

Imagine picking up a book to read and the first five chapters are blank. Throughout this book, there are gaps and missing paragraphs in each chapter. That is what an adoptee's story is like—at least an adoptee with little or no information regarding themselves or their biological family. If I had to categorize my story, it would fall under mystery. I had to figure out the when, who, and the why.

There are adoptees that have no interest in searching for their biological families, which is fine. My inquisitive and curious nature is what propelled me to uncover the answers to all my questions. If you are someone interested in searching, just beginning a search, or in the midst of one, I encourage you to not give up. There are no guarantees in life. I was lucky—if you call over thirty years of searching lucky. When I started on my personal pilgrimage into the unknown, I did not have a single name. I started with nothing but my date of birth and the city where I was born. I worked hard, persevered, and in the end I did not give up—although I must admit, I thought about it many times. Being adopted can mean different things to different people, but there are two common questions that most of us share: Who? Why?

I was once asked if I feel differently about myself now that my journey has come to the end. The answer is a resounding, yes! Of course I do. I needed to connect my past to my present. I have now learned why I look and always felt different, why I had that great void in my life. The feeling that something was always missing is no longer a part of who I am. I may not have the answers to all of my questions, but I do have more that I ever thought possible. I feel fulfilled. I feel blessed. I feel complete.

For so many years, I felt less than whole. I was determined to find out why. Maybe if I had felt that I had fit in with my adopted family and had not felt like an outsider, then I would not have been driven to search. It has been noted that physical and emotional characteristics help children define themselves and their connection to others. Finding similarity in others gives us comfort. We all need the feeling that we belong somewhere and our securities are nurtured by looking like those around us. It is important that an adoptee has physical and emotional attachments to their adopted families. I did not have either of those.

I strongly believe that each and every one of us has the right to know who we are and where we come from. Not being allowed access to that information, our birth records, is not only unjust, it goes against our civil rights and can have a tremendous negative impact. The State of New York did not share that I had three older brothers when I had applied for the Non-Identifying Information. But for some reason, I did not accept that. I had such a strong sense that I did indeed have a sibling. So, I continued to search. I just did not realize how many siblings.

The State is legally allowed to release to an adoptee the knowledge of any existing siblings. It would be twelve long years before I discovered on my own that I had three brothers. Would my search for my siblings have started much sooner? Of course it would have. Was I obsessed with searching? Sometimes yes, and sometimes no, but I was determined to see it through to the end, regardless of the outcome.

My journey began by writing a letter in 1986 to the State of New York. It included more telephone calls and hours spent on the computer than I could ever count. I traveled to towns and cities in hope of finding anything that would help me discover any bit of information regarding my family. Each and every time I share my personal story; I still experience the exact same emotions as I did at the time of the specific event. I relive each and every feeling the same today as I did five, ten, or twenty years ago. They never go away. When I hear another adoptee's story, I react the same: I feel their joy, pain, excitement, fear, and disappointment all as if they were happening to me.

There have been other family dinners with my brothers. Charles and John and I speak on the phone. Rick and

I see each other frequently. His daughter, Andrea, now works for Paul. My three brothers and I have missed out on a lifetime of knowing each other. We do not have childhood memories to share, but we are connected by chance and by a woman who none of us knew or will ever understand. She will always remain an enigma. I hold no animosity towards Margaret. She did what she felt she had to do.

It's funny, but something as simple as choosing a birthday card to send to one of my siblings is daunting and time-consuming. The majority of cards reference something from a past that was shared or mention growing up together. My brothers, my sisters, and I have no past together, but we do have a present and a future.

I had always focused on finding and having siblings. But I had not put much thought or consideration into the fact that at the same time I found a sibling, I also became someone's sibling. I was a daughter, wife, mother, aunt, sister-in-law, cousin, and niece, but never a sibling. So I had to ask myself, how do I learn to be a sister? I don't have an answer to that. All I have come up with is that I can be a good friend, one who happens to be related.

My sister Kim and I are in touch and see each other several times a year. Natalie and I speak frequently and see each other when I am in Saratoga. A couple of years ago on a Saturday morning, Paul and I decided to go see our horse that is kept on a farm outside Saratoga in the winter. We were driving out to the farm and suddenly realized that the farm is down the road from where Natalie lives. She has been a neighbor to our trainer for years. As I have said before, it is indeed, a very small world.

At the age of sixty-four, I finally know my father's name and what he looked like. That was one part of my story I thought would always remain a mystery. I will always be indebted to Sandy for all her time and hard work in making the discovery. And now, on my paternal side, I have names and information going all the way back to the 1600s.

Through a lot of investigating I have recently learned and pieced together a few more details about my birth mother's family. Aside from Aunt Bea being Margaret's biological mother, Robert Taggart was really her father. This also means that all the research I had done years ago on the Taggart family is in fact part of my family tree.

My adopted mother passed away at the age of ninety-five on July 31, 2015. She went to her grave with her BIG SECRET. She never shared the story of my adoption. Due to her deteriorating health issues from congestive heart failure, in January of 2015 I had no option but to put her into a nursing home—one of the most agonizing decisions I have ever had to make. It was hell for me and for her. Although she had always been a very tough person, I never witnessed such behavior from her as I did when she was placed in the nursing home. She was furious with me, she swore which I had never heard her do, and was not pleasant to the staff. I would constantly tell her how sorry I was that she ended up in a nursing home and asked her what other options were there? I had tried in-home care but she needed round-the-clock care. I still live with the guilt.

Everyone at the nursing home tried with my mother. I knew someone who worked there and she was so kind and would visit my mother every week. One day, her daughter came with her to visit my mother. She grew up with my son Jeff and had met my mother several times throughout the years. Her mom said to her, "Susan doesn't look at all like Priscilla."

"Mom, you don't know? Susan is adopted!"

My mother's social worker would try to talk to her, and one day she sat down with me to discuss my mother. During my conversation with the social worker, I told her a little of my story. She told me that I should bring the subject up with my mother before it was too late. I told her I was afraid to. I thought about talking to her many times, especially over the past seven months of her life, but I never quite knew how to start the conversation. I always had such anxiety and was so apprehensive when I thought about it. But one day I found the courage to speak to her and told her what I had discovered. I told her everything.

It was Friday, July 31 and when I arrived at the nursing home that morning, she wasn't doing well. She seemed to be drifting in and out of consciousness and the end of her life seemed near. So on this day, sitting on a chair across the small room from where she was lying on her bed, I started the long overdue conversation. I said I had something important to tell her and started by telling her that I had three brothers and a sister. I told her I was angry with her for not ever allowing me to talk about my adoption. I told her I was sad that she never wanted to be a part of this and I hated her keeping everything a secret.

Yes, I finally did it. After all the years, after all the discoveries and events in my life, I told her my story. I do not know what she heard and understood. But I will say that it was cathartic for me. A great burden had been lifted. There it was—my BIG SECRET was a secret no more.

I sat staring at her for a couple of hours. She would moan and try to talk but I couldn't understand what she was trying to say. It was sad to watch. When it came time for me to leave, I stood up and lingered in the doorway for quite awhile, looking at her before saying goodbye. I told her that I would see her later, but I never did. She died a little past eight o'clock that evening.

I went from being that "lonely child" standing by the window on Sunday afternoons peering through the sheer faded fabric curtain, yearning to have a family like the one living next door, to now having one. I have my husband, my children, my grandchildren, my much-wanted siblings—in fact, more siblings than I could ever imagine. I have nieces, nephews, sisters-in-law, brothers-in-law, cousins, and even ancestors. I am now not the tallest person in the family photographs. I now know why I am not "five-foot-two with eyes of blue." In fact, I have grown to like my green Irish eyes.

Everyone is on a personal journey in life, and this was mine. For whatever reason, I was meant to go on this journey, to trace my origins back as much as I could and to discover from whom and where I came. It still amazes me that I was able to muddle through and unearth as much as I did, and for that I am eternally grateful. With the recent discovery of my birth father and the addition of more siblings and an extensive family tree on both my birth parents' sides, I find it hard to believe that there would be much left to discover, but again, who knows?

I am truly amazed when I look at the family tree that

I now have. Am I done searching? Well, I believe so, but never, say never. I know there's a possibility that there could be a few more siblings out there somewhere.

When I sat down to write the ending of my story, I realized that maybe at this point in my life I really can't. Maybe my journey of search isn't quite over. But at this particular point in my life, I am at peace with everything I have discovered. From where I began to where I am now, I can't help but think it's pretty remarkable.

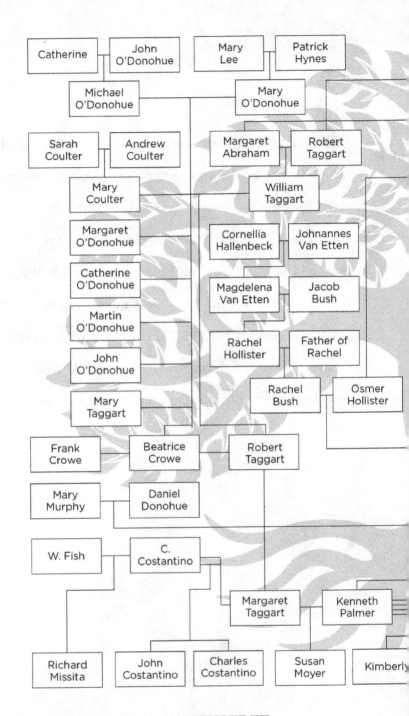

BIOLOGICAL FAMILY TREE

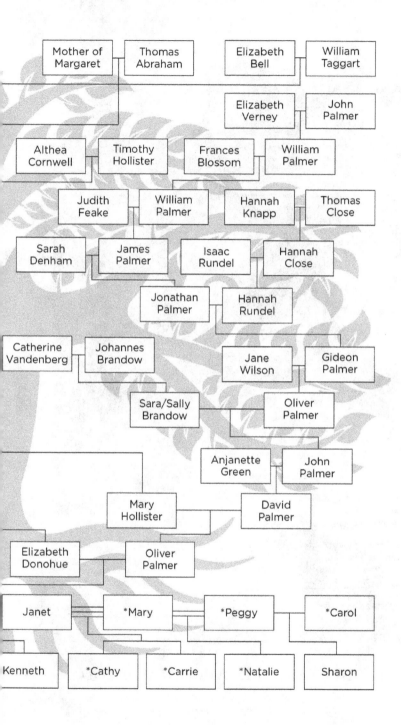

YOUNG MARGARET AT CONEY ISLAND

WITH MY DOLL (LEFT)

MY MOTHER WITH HER DOLL (RIGHT)

BEATRICE WITH YOUNG JOHN AND CHARLES

JEFFREY AND JASON MOYER

KENNETH'S GRAVE

KENNETH AND HIS DOG "PRINCESS"

MY HUSBAND, PAUL MOYER

ACKNOWLEDGMENTS

Much gratitude to my friends and family who kept telling me that I should write a book. I believe the main reason is because no one could keep the facts, events, and all my discoveries of new family members straight.

For Paul, my biggest supporter, who knew me when I was that only "lonely child" without any siblings, or so I thought. You have been by my side throughout this long journey that seems neverending. Thank you for your love, support, and encouragement each step of the way. Although every time I say, "Guess what?" you say, "I know, you found a new relative," each time you are truly happy for me.

To my siblings, many cousins, and newfound relatives, thank you for accepting me into your lives. Words cannot express how much it means to me.

And many thanks to the staff of Dream Your Book:

My editor Nina Alvarez, who first heard my story a number of years ago and convinced me that I really did have a story to tell and told me that I could do it. It's only been possible with your help and guidance. Thanks for keeping the faith.

Carolyn Birrittella for your PR wisdom and experience and for listening to me at the times when I was most overwhelmed and discouraged.

Copyeditor Raquel Pidal for being that all-important last pair of eyes.

And finally, to designer Rachael Gootnik, who I know that I drove absolutely crazy when trying to explain my family tree. It is certainly not your average tree.

ABOUT THE AUTHOR

Susan Moyer was born in Albany, New York and grew up in Syracuse, New York. She had a career in advertising and radio for many years as a copy writer, creative director, and radio commercial producer. Later she worked in special education. Susan is an author, speaker, and supporter and proponent for Adoptee Equal Rights. She has been married for thirty-eight years to her husband, Paul, and lives in Rochester, New York where they raised their two sons.

BIO MOYER

Moyer, Susan
The lonely child : the
journey of search to

11/23/20

9 780692 125076